Issues in contemporary theology
Series Editor: I. H. Marshall

The present-day Christological debate

In this series

The origins of New Testament Christology
I. Howard Marshall

The search for salvation
David F. Wells

Christian hope and the future of man
Stephen H. Travis

Theology encounters revolution
J. Andrew Kirk

Approaches to Old Testament interpretation
John Goldingay

THE PRESENT-DAY CHRISTOLOGICAL DEBATE

Klaas Runia

Inter-Varsity Press

INTER-VARSITY PRESS
38 De Montfort Street, Leicester LE1 7GP, England
Box 1400, Downers Grove, IL 60515, U.S.A.

© *Klaas Runia 1984*

Unless otherwise stated, quotations from the Bible are from the Revised Standard Version, copyrighted 1946, 1952, © 1971, 1973, by the Division of Christian Education, National Council of the Churches of Christ in the USA, and used by permission.

Inter-Varsity Press, England, is the publishing division of the Universities and Colleges Christian Fellowship (formerly the Inter-Varsity Fellowship), a student movement linking Christian Unions in universities and colleges throughout the United Kingdom and the Republic of Ireland, and a member movement of the International Fellowship of Evangelical Students. For information about local and national activities write to UCCF, 38 De Montfort Street, Leicester LE1 7GP.

InterVarsity Press, U.S.A., is the book-publishing division of Inter-Varsity Christian Fellowship, a student movement active on campus at hundreds of universities, colleges and schools of nursing. For information about local and regional activities, write IVCF, 233 Langdon St., Madison, WI 53703.

Distributed in Canada through InterVarsity Press, 860 Denison St., Unit 3, Markham, Ontario L3R 4H1, Canada.

Phototypeset by Input Typesetting Ltd, London
Printed in the United States of America

British Library Cataloguing in Publication Data
Runia, Klaas
    The present-day Christological debate.
    –(Issues in contemporary theology)
    1.   Jesus Christ
    I.   Title   II. Series
    232   BT202
    ISBN 0-85111-405-9

Library of Congress Cataloging in Publication Data

Runia, K. (Klaas), 1926-
    The present-day Christological debate.

    (Issues in contemporary theology)
    Includes bibliographical references.
    1.   Jesus Christ–History of doctrines–20th century.
I.   Title.   II. Series.
BT198.R86   1984   232   84-6554
ISBN 0-87784-937-4

16	15	14	13	12	11	10	9	8	7	6	5	4	3	2	1
97	96	95	94	93	92	91	90	89	88	87	86	85	84		

General Preface

'Issues in contemporary theology' is a series of short books which survey and discuss issues of current biblical and theological interest. All the subjects are of theological importance and arouse considerable controversy among scholars of different outlooks. Students may often be confused by the variety of opinions with which they are confronted in their lectures and reading lists, so that the study of a particular subject may well leave them more perplexed than when they started. In such a situation it is valuable to have an over-view of the subject before starting detailed study, so that they may have some idea of where they are going and some guidance to aid them in making their own judgments.

It is not only theological students who need such help; they must study such subjects as are treated in this series as part of their professional training. Many other people will be interested to listen in to what the theologians are talking about, since ultimately what the theologians say affects what preachers and popular writers communicate to a wider audience, and they in turn help to mould the thinking, attitudes and actions of society at large. It is greatly to be desired that Christians in general should be able to evaluate for themselves what the theologians say. Such people will welcome reliable, succinct guides to current theological thinking.

The purpose of the series is, then, to trace a path through the tangled undergrowth of theological discussion so that the student may have some idea of the route and the destination, the alluring sidepaths and the recommended road. What is offered here is no more than a path, and at times it may seem decidedly slippery and even precipitous. Nor does the writer necessarily follow it straight to the goal. He will stop to explore the sidepaths, if only to show that they are dead ends; he will pause to examine the interesting

5

objects to be found on the way. At most what he can offer is a guidebook, based on his own travels, for the benefit of future explorers who will have to make their own way with its aid, perhaps correcting the map in places, perhaps confirming its accuracy in others, often clearing away the jungle that has encroached on the right path since it was last used. But each contributor to the series believes that a path does exist; he has tried it out himself, and believes that it leads to the destination, even if the exact nature of the destination is not obvious until one has travelled a long way.

Some Christians see little value in the kind of discussion attempted in these books, and even theological students have been known to regard such study as a dreary duty valuable only as an aid to passing examinations. They may think that, since their system of theology is the right one, there is no point in studying writings from other points of view. Such an attitude would be misguided. None of us has a monopoly of the truth and all of us can learn even from those with whom we may most profoundly disagree. One may indeed be stimulated far more to reach fresh insights into the truth by reading provocative statements from different schools of thought than by ploughing through more pedestrian expositions of one's own point of view. If we believe that the Lord has yet more light and truth to break forth from his Holy Word, we shall all the more gladly enter into a creative encounter with writers expressive of different opinions and seek to re-form our own understanding in accordance with that Word. An evangelical stance in theology can be both critical of other points of view and also self-critical. It is the prayer of all who are concerned with the production of this series that these books may help students of all shades of opinion to come to a deeper understanding of the truth as it is in Jesus.

I. HOWARD MARSHALL

Contents

Author's Preface

The substance of this book was originally prepared as a paper for the Third Conference of the Fellowship of European Evangelical Theologians, held in 1980 at the New Life Centre, Wölmersen, West-Germany. The general theme of the conference was: *Who is Jesus Christ? The Modern Challenges for Christology.* This theme was chosen because of the fact that in recent years the doctrine of Christ has become the focal point of theological discussion. In many respects our days resemble the early centuries of the Christian church, when the great Christological debate took place, finally issuing in the decisions of the Councils of Nicea (325), Constantinople (381), Ephesus (431) and Chalcedon (451). Today the question, 'Who is Jesus?' is again asked, and many leading theologians of our day voice the opinion that the classical answers are inadequate and that new answers must be found and given. Naturally, evangelical theologians are deeply interested in this debate. They believe that Jesus is the Son of God, who came down from heaven 'for us and for our salvation' (Nicene Creed). But they cannot avoid the challenges that issue from the present Christological debate.

At the request of the Editor of this series I have expanded the original paper into this book. From the table of contents the reader can see that I have restricted myself to developments within Western, mainly European, theology. Developments in Asian and African theology are usually of quite a different nature, because here the classical Christology is challenged, not from within but from without, namely by the questions posed by other world religions.

I hope that this book will help to give theological students, ministers and other interested Christians something of a bird's-eye view of the debate that is still going on. Above all I hope that the readers may be strengthened in their personal faith in Jesus Christ as their

God-given Saviour and Lord. The book deals with the very heart of the Christian faith. Our discussion opens with a general question: 'Who do *men* say that I am?' (Mk. 8:27). But the decisive question, which the reader has to answer for himself, is 'Who do *you* say that I am?' (Mk. 8:29).

Finally, I want to express my indebtedness to my youngest son, Anthony Peter Runia, for reading the entire manuscript and suggesting many linguistic improvements.

Chapter One

'Who do men say that I am?'

One of the most crucial moments in the Gospels is Peter's confession: 'You are the Christ, the Son of the living God' (Mt. 16:16; *cf*. Mk. 8:29; Lk. 9:20). Jesus himself calls for this confession. He knows that people often talk about him and that many regard him as an extraordinary person. This is shown by the answer to the first question he asks: 'Who do *men* say that the Son of man is?' The answer given by the disciples indicates that there is a great variety of opinions among the people: 'Some say John the Baptist, others say Elijah, and others Jeremiah or one of the prophets.' Then Jesus goes on to ask: 'But who do *you* say that I am?' This is the heart of the matter. In the final analysis every one has to give his own personal answer and make his own personal confession.

In recent years this question has again been very much at the centre of theological discussion, as appears from the fact that a great number of important studies in Christology have been published. The answers given, however, are generally quite different from the one given by the Christian church throughout the centuries.

The ancient church

The great battle over Christology was fought in the ancient church. We cannot trace the complicated course of the whole battle here.[1] It must suffice to mention the important decisions of some of the ecumenical councils. First of all, the Council of Nicea (AD 325) stated that Jesus is the Son of God in the full sense of the word. The key word in its confession was *homoousios*, *i.e.* Jesus is 'of the same substance' with the Father. This was a non-biblical term (which previously had been used even by unorthodox people!), but the Council Fathers felt that they should use it, because it so clearly and

---

[1] For a full account, see Gerald Bray, *Creeds, Councils and Christ*, 1984.

11

unambiguously expressed what they understood to be the teaching of Scripture.[2] Later on, in the so-called Nicene Creed,[3] the same doctrine was stated in the following words:

> I believe in one Lord Jesus Christ, the only-begotten Son of God, begotten of the Father before all worlds; God of God, Light of Light, very God of very God; begotten, not made, being of one substance (*homoousion*) with the Father, by whom all things were made.

But the Creed stresses not only his divinity but also his humanity, for it continues:

> Who . . . was incarnate by the Holy Spirit of the Virgin Mary, and was made man.

Thus Nicea confessed: *very God* and *very man*.

This confession, however, immediately raised new questions. How are these two statements related? How can one person be both God and man? The Council of Chalcedon (AD 451) answered this question by speaking of one (divine) Person and two natures: a divine and a human nature:

> We confess . . . one and the same Christ, Son, Lord, Only-begotten, to be acknowledged of two natures, *without confusion, without change, without division, without separation*; the distinction of natures being in no wise done away because of the union, but rather the characteristic property of each nature being preserved, and concurring into one Person, . . . not as if Christ were parted or divided into two Persons, but one and the same Son and Only-begotten God, Lord, Jesus Christ.

The church has always been aware that this too was an inadequate formulation. It realized full well that the being of Jesus Christ is a mystery. This was also the reason why to a large extent the statement of Chalcedon was put in a negative form. The Fathers, so to speak,

---

[2] We shall address this crucial question at the conclusion of our survey in ch. 9, below.

[3] 'So-called', because the present form of the Creed does not date from the Council of Nicea but from that of Constantinople, AD 381.

put up four fences (without confusion, without change, without division, without separation) and said: The mystery lies within this area. At the same time they were deeply convinced that, despite the inadequacies of the formulation, the decision expressed the truth about Jesus, namely that he is very God and very man in one Person.

In the following centuries the church adhered to the statements of Nicea, Constantinople and Chalcedon. Even the division between the Eastern and Western churches (AD 1054) did not change this; both churches retained the Christology of the early church. Likewise the Reformation, the great division within the Western church, left the situation unchanged. All major Reformation churches (Lutheran, Reformed, Anglican) accepted the ancient creeds. It was only in the eighteenth century that serious opposition arose from the new liberal theology, but even then the churches themselves, at least officially, retained the old Christological dogma. As far as I know, none of the historic churches has ever officially abandoned it. One may even say that throughout this whole period and also in our own century it remained the shibboleth that distinguished orthodoxy from liberalism.

The new challenge

In recent years, however, we observe the remarkable fact that the ancient dogma is opposed by people who up till now were never regarded as liberal. Many contemporary theologians, from both orthodox Protestant and Roman Catholic backgrounds, are of the opinion that the Christology of the ancient creeds is no longer tenable.

This new opposition is the more remarkable since from the twenties of this century onward there had been a revival of the classical high Christology in the theology of Karl Barth. For more than twenty-five years Barth's theology dominated the theological scene. His theology was a strong reaction against the older liberal theology of the nineteenth century and the early decades of this century, with its strong emphasis on the religious nature of man himself. Over against this anthropocentrism Barth put his Christocentrism, which, according to him, was fully in conformity with the New Testament itself.

After World War 2 a reaction set in, focusing on the anthropological aspect of the Christian faith. In German theology this became known as '*die anthropologische Wende*' (the anthropological shift).

The central question now was: How can we interpret the Christian message in such a way that modern man can recognize it as something that is of vital importance to him? Within this framework of thought the Christology of the ancient creeds became increasingly problematic for many theologians.

The main issue for them is that these creeds fail to do justice to the person of Jesus as he comes to us from the pages of the New Testament, in particular of the Gospels. The creeds see Jesus as someone who combines Godhead and manhood in one person. But is this really the picture of Jesus as we see it in the Gospels? Moreover, is such a combination of Godhead and manhood in one person really possible? Is Jesus in this case still a real man, one of us and one like us? Taking these questions as their cue, many leading theologians of our day have tried to develop a new Christology, which takes its starting-point not in a divine Person who took manhood upon himself, but in the historical Jesus, the man Jesus as he was here on earth among us. In doing this they do not deny that he was a very special man, unique among all men. On the contrary, they all affirm this. But at the same time they also want to emphasize that he was a *man*, a *real* man. His uniqueness was his unique *human* relationship with God. Because of this relationship he can be called *the* revelation and representation of God in this world. But at the same time we must maintain that it was a *human* revelation and representation, and no more.

From this brief introduction it is already clear that there are several factors which have prompted the new developments in Christological thought. It may be helpful, even at this early stage, to spell them out a little more explicitly. I think that at least the following three matters must be mentioned, because they are found – albeit with a differing degree of emphasis – in nearly every modern Christology.

In the first place there is the *exegetical* angle. It is claimed that modern historical-critical exegesis of the New Testament has shown that there is a plurality of Christologies within the New Testament; therefore it is not correct to say that one particular Christology, namely, the high, incarnational Christology of the creeds, is *the* New Testament Christology.

Secondly, it is argued that the creeds as they stand are not only couched in the Greek *philosophical language* of the early centuries, but are also deeply influenced and contaminated by the *metaphysical modes of thinking* of that period. For this reason the Christology of the creeds cannot be regarded as *the* Christology which is binding on the church of all ages.

Thirdly, we are told that the ancient Christology does not mean anything to people of this age. We no longer think primarily in *ontological* categories, but modern thinking is *functional* in nature. The basic question is not: 'Who is Jesus Christ and what, therefore, has he done for us?', but rather: 'What has he done and who, therefore, is he for us?' Moreover, can we really visualize anything at all, when we use such terms as 'incarnation'? Or, to put it in the words of M. Wiles: 'Are we sure that the concept of an incarnate being, one who is both fully God and fully man, is after all an intelligible concept?'[4]

In the following pages we shall make an attempt to trace some of the main lines of development in Christological thought in recent years. It will prove to be a rather intricate pattern, for even in the case of similarity of approach there are many variations. We shall also see that the different emphases in Christology have far-reaching consequences for the rest of theology, in particular for the doctrine of God.

[4] M. Wiles, in *The Myth of God Incarnate*, ed. John Hick, 1978, p. 5.

Chapter Two

Karl Barth

Our survey begins, then, with the towering figure of Karl Barth whose influence has been felt throughout Western theology in the twentieth century. For him the whole subject of Christology was central to theology, and in conscious reaction to the liberal theology of the preceding century he affirmed the classical orthodox statements of the first five centuries on the person of Christ. Shifts were to take place in his thinking, as we shall see, and these have been developed by later theologians beyond the bounds of traditional orthodoxy. But throughout his long career Barth himself adhered faithfully to the classical Christology, and the shifts in his thinking always took place within that framework.

Herbert Hartwell's introduction to Barth's theology includes a chapter on Jesus Christ with the following heading: 'Jesus Christ, the Key to the Understanding of God, the Universe and Man'.[1] This is no exaggeration. Especially since his study of 1931 on *Anselm: Fides Quaerens Intellectum*[2] Barth was bent upon a thorough-going Christological concentration of the whole range of systematic theology. In the first volume of his *Church Dogmatics* he wrote: 'A church dogmatics must, of course, be christologically determined as a whole and in all its parts, as surely as the revealed Word of God, attested by Holy Scripture and proclaimed by the Church, is its one and only criterion, and as surely as this revealed Word is identical with Jesus Christ. If dogmatics cannot regard itself and cause itself to be regarded as fundamentally Christology, it has assuredly succumbed to some alien sway and is already on the verge of losing its character as church dogmatics.'[3]

[1] Herbert Hartwell, *The Theology of Karl Barth, An Introduction*, 1964, p. 95.
[2] First English edition in 1960.
[3] *Church Dogmatics (CD)* I, 2, p. 123. *Cf. Dogmatics in Outline*, 1958, pp. 39, 65f. On p. 66 Barth says that Christology is the touchstone of all knowledge of God in the Christian sense, the touchstone of all theology. 'Tell me how it stands with your Christology, and I shall tell who you are'.

16

According to Barth, Jesus Christ is the beginning of all God's ways and works. Everything starts with God's election of the God-man Jesus Christ. For this same reason everything else must be seen in the light of Jesus Christ. This is true of the doctrine of creation (*CD* III, 1), of anthropology (III, 2), of providence (III, 3), of election (II, 2) and also of the doctrine of God himself (II, 1). It is therefore not surprising that at times Barth has been accused of 'Christomonism'. His entire eleven-volume *Church Dogmatics* is one long explanation and unfolding of this one name, Jesus Christ.

When we further ask: Who is Jesus Christ for Barth?, we find that in his view of the person of Christ he stays firmly within the framework of the classical, orthodox theology. Without any hesitation he accepts the Christology of the ancient church.[4] 'The central statement of the Christology of the Ancient Church is that God becomes one with man: Jesus Christ "Very God and very man".'[5] The last words are from the statement of the Council of Chalcedon about the two natures of Christ. Barth fully accepts this statement and rejects the charge of intellectualism that had been levelled against it by such scholars as Herder and Harnack. Indeed, he turns the tables on them and accuses them of spiritualistic moralism.[6] The Council, on the other hand, cannot be faulted with intellectualism, for 'in speaking of the two natures, of the *vere Deus* and the *vere homo*, in the one Person of Jesus Christ, it did not intend to solve the mystery of revelation, but rather it perceived and respected this mystery'.[7] One can also say that the formula of Chalcedon is actually nothing else than an exegesis of John 1:14 – '*Ho Logos sarx egeneto*' – The Word became flesh.[8]

First of all this phrase says that Jesus is *vere Deus*, for he is the *Word*. But Jesus is also *vere homo*, for the Word became *flesh*. Finally we must also stress the word 'became'. This does not mean that the Word changed into a man and ceased to be what he is in himself. Neither does it mean a third kind of being, midway between God and man. No, he takes a human nature upon himself *in addition to* a divine nature.

Barth even defends such abstract terms as '*anhypostatos*' and '*enhypostatos*'. Both terms, coined in the sixth century, belong together and actually are two aspects of the same reality. The '*anhypostatos*' stresses the negative aspect by affirming that the human nature of

[4] *Cf.* his exposition of the Nicene Creed, *CD* I, 1, pp. 48ff.
[5] *CD* I, 2, p. 125.   [6] *Ibid.*, p. 130.
[7] *Ibid.*, p. 129.   [8] *Ibid.*, pp. 132ff.

Christ had no separate '*hypostasis*' of its own, that is, it did not exist apart from the Son of God who assumed the human nature. The '*enhypostatos*' emphasizes the positive aspect by affirming that from its very beginning the Logos was the '*hypostasis*' of the human nature. For Barth this doctrine is not just an abstruse, hyper-theological formulation, but it is 'particularly well adapted to make it clear that . . . Jesus Christ is the reality of a divine act of Lordship which is unique and singular as compared with all other events'.[9] This doctrine clearly indicates that in the incarnation the initiative comes from God's side. Later on, in his doctrine of reconciliation, Barth calls this formula 'the sum and root of all the graces addressed to Him'.[10]

There can be no doubt that in all this Barth is fully in agreement with the Christology of the ancient church. In fact, due to him there arose a revival of interest in and acceptance of the ancient Christology in many circles which for a long time had been very critical or even negative. Following Barth, many were willing to accept even the virgin birth again.[11]

It is not surprising either that Barth also wholeheartedly accepted the classical doctrine of the Trinity. In fact, it is so important and so central for him that he deals with it in the very first volume of his *Church Dogmatics*, where he discusses the doctrine of revelation or the Word of God. This revelation not only took place in Jesus Christ who is the Word of God, but it also confronts us directly with God as the Triune God. 'If we mean by the word "revelation" "the Word became flesh and dwelt among us", then we are asserting something that is to be grounded only within the Trinity; namely, by the will of the Father, by the mission of the Son and of the Holy Spirit, by the eternal decree of the Triune God, i.e., not otherwise than as the knowledge of God from God, as knowledge of the Light in the Light.'[12] If Jesus Christ really is the revelation of God, then there is a God who is revealed by him, and if the revelation of God in and through Jesus Christ is to be really effective, then God himself must bring this revelation home to man, the sinner. Three times it is God himself who is the Subject of his own Word. He is the Revealer, the Revelation and the Revealedness. This can only mean that God is Triune, that 'God Himself in unimpaired unity yet also in unimpaired difference is Revealer, Revelation and Revealedness'.[13]

[9] *Ibid.*, p. 165.   [10] *CD* IV, 2, p. 91.   [11] *Cf. CD* I, 2, pp. 173–202.
[12] *CD* I, 1, p. 134.   [13] *Ibid.*, p. 339.

Barth further strongly emphasizes that God is Triune in his innermost Being. It is not sufficient to accept an 'economic' Trinity, *i.e.*, God manifests himself as such only in the history of the world, but we have to proceed to the 'ontological' or 'essential' Trinity, *i.e.*, God is Triune in his innermost Being. 'The reality of God in his revelation is not to be bracketed with an "only", as though somewhere behind his revelation there stood another reality of God, but the reality of God which meets us in revelation is reality in all the depths of eternity.'[14]

No wonder that for Barth the divinity of Jesus Christ belongs to the very centre of the Christian faith. In fact, in the earlier volumes of the *Church Dogmatics* it receives so much emphasis that Barth has been accused of identifying Jesus with God to such an extent that his humanity recedes into the background and there is hardly any place left for an 'over against' of Jesus and God.[15] Jesus is so much on the side of God that his humanity is almost dwarfed into insignificance. His cry on the cross, 'My God, my God, why hast thou forsaken me?', is interpreted in a manner that suggests that the battle is actually fought within the Godhead himself.

Yet Barth does not really want to go so far. He emphatically rejects the idea of 'a contradiction and conflict in God Himself' and even calls such an idea the 'supreme blasphemy'.[16] On the other hand, there is also the fact that he reiterates time and again that it is not the man Jesus who brings about the reconciliation of man with God, but that it is the act of God in him. G. C. Berkouwer has pointed out how this idea is presented by Barth in a great variety of ways.[17] For instance, Barth speaks of the self-surrender of God, of God's endangering himself, of the humiliation of God, of the self-sacrifice of God, of the passion of God, *etc.* (The only expression that is not used by Barth is the 'death' of God!) It is not surprising that in this connection Berkouwer himself raises the question whether Barth is not guilty of a new form of theopaschitism.[18] 'When Barth speaks of the suffering of God and even of an "obedience of God", and this not as a bold manner of speaking but as an *essential* element in the being of God . . . , he exceeds the boundaries of the

---

[14] *Ibid.*, p. 548.
[15] *Cf.* A. van de Beek, *De menselijke persoon van Christus*, 1980, p. 54.
[16] *CD* IV, 1, p. 185.
[17] G. C. Berkouwer, *The Triumph of Grace in the Theology of Karl Barth*, 1956, p. 127.
[18] *Ibid.*, pp. 125–135, 297–327.

revelation which we have in Christ. . . . To conclude . . . to a tension and an obedience in God Himself, to an "above" and a "below" in Him, can only be characterized as speculation.'[19]

The Christian church has always avoided this danger by speaking emphatically of the Son *in his human nature*.[20] The contrast is not between Father and Son as such, it is not an inter-trinitarian contrast or tension, but the Son in his human form subjects himself to the Father. Barth definitely goes beyond this when he says that the Gospels speak of the passion of Jesus 'as an act of God which is coincident with the free action and suffering of a man, but in such a way that this human action and suffering has to be represented and understood as the action and, therefore, the passion of God Himself'.[21] As we shall see later on, this approach of Barth has been influential in shaping the Christology of J. Moltmann and others. They not only share Barth's idea of the suffering of God, but go even far beyond it by also speaking of death in God.

There is, however, another line of thought in Barth's Christology which we must pursue a little further. In later years we see a *certain shift* taking place in Barth's thinking. He still maintains that it is God who is the real Subject in the revelation that took place in Jesus Christ, but now the emphasis is much more on Jesus who is the true representative of mankind and who as such acts as the human partner of God.

In his paper on *The humanity of God* which was delivered in 1956[22] Barth gave a public account of this shift in emphasis. The central concept is the covenant God made with man. 'In his one person Jesus Christ is just as much as true *God* of *man* as as true *man* of *God* the faithful partner, just as much the Lord humiliated for fellowship with man as the servant elevated into the fellowship with God . . . , both unconfused but also undivided, fully the one and fully the other. So, in this unity, Jesus Christ is the Mediator,

---

[19] *Ibid.*, p. 304.
[20] Cf. the *Heidelberg Catechism*, Answer 37: 'That throughout his life on earth, but especially at the end of it, he bore *in body and soul* the wrath of God against the sin of the whole human race . . .'. Cf. *Reformed Confessions of the Sixteenth Century*, ed. Arthur Cochrane, 1966, p. 311.
[21] *CD* IV, 1, p. 245. On the next page, however, Barth says it differently and more in conformity with the church's traditional view: 'It is the eternal God Himself who has given Himself in His Son to be man and as man to take upon Himself this human passion'. The comparison of these two statements shows that there is a strong, if not insoluble, tension at this point in Barth's Christology.
[22] It was published in English in 1965, tr. J. N. Thomas and T. Wieser.

the Reconciler of God and man. So He represents God with man, commanding and rousing faith, love and hope – and so He represents man with God by his substitution, satisfaction and intercession.'[23]

In a similar way Barth writes in his *Evangelical Theology: An Introduction*: 'Through His Word God discloses His work in His *covenant* with man. . . . He discloses Himself as the *primary* partner of the covenant – Himself as *man*'s God. But He also discloses *man* to be His creature. . . . He discloses man as God's man, as God's son and servant who is loved by Him. Man is thus the other, the secondary, partner of the covenant'.[24] And where do we find this disclosure? It is 'the Word which God *has spoken*, *still speaks* and will *speak again* in the history of Jesus Christ which fulfils the history of Israel'. In other words, Jesus Christ is the true partner of God and it is only through him that all other men can be partners of God.

As we shall see later on, this line of thought in Barth's Christology is taken up again in several recent Christological concepts, such as those of E. Flesseman and H. Berkhof. But we shall also see that in their concepts the idea of Jesus Christ as God's true partner undergoes a complete and essential change. In the case of Barth himself we cannot speak of such an essential change. In Barth there is only a shift in emphasis within a framework that essentially remains the same. Even when Jesus is seen as the true partner of God, he is such only as the Son of God who became flesh. It is, therefore, not surprising to see that in the same volume in which he speaks of this partnership, Barth again upholds and defends the doctrine of the '*anhypostatos*' and the '*enhypostatos*' and states: 'It is only as the Son of God that Jesus Christ also exists as man'.[25]

As Barth's influence was at its zenith, new trends were emerging of a much more radical nature that were to take Western theology along a road that led far from the orthodox position of the ancient church. It is to these that we now turn.

---

[23] *Die Menschlichkeit Gottes*, 1956, p. 11 (my own translation). Identical ideas were already present in the second volume on reconciliation, *CD* IV, 2, which was published in 1955.
[24] Quoted in Barth's *Evangelical Theology: An Introduction*, 1963, pp. 19f.
[25] *CD* IV, 2, p. 91.

Chapter Three

New developments

Rudolf Bultmann

After World War 2 a shift took place as Rudolf Bultmann's programme of demythologizing and his existentialist interpretation of
the biblical message became the new centre of theological discussion.
For Bultmann, the cross of Jesus was the centre of all theology, but
his approach to the cross and to the person of Jesus himself was
decisively different from that of Barth in at least two ways.

First of all, Bultmann approached the New Testament from a
radical critical point of view. As one of the fathers of the form-
critical school, he believed that the New Testament writings do not
describe factual history, but rather are the products of the theology
of the early Christian communities. In the process of oral transmis-
sion and regular preaching all kinds of legendary elements were
added to the original history of Jesus.

Furthermore, as a representative of the religio-historical school,
Bultmann also saw a close relationship between the New Testament
message and the non-Christian religions of that period. Here he
found the background of the mythological interpretations of Jesus
and his death and resurrection, as given by the New Testament
writers. In his analysis of the titles 'God and Saviour', ascribed to
Jesus in the confessional basis of the World Council of Churches,
he found a double background for the expression 'Son of God'. In
the primitive Palestinian community the term simply meant to say
that Jesus is the Messiah, the eschatological bringer of salvation.[1] In
Hellenistic Christendom the same title indicates the divine quality
of Jesus[2] and his being looked upon as a divine figure.[3] Yet in this

[1] Rudolf Bultmann, 'The Christological Confession of the World Council of
Church', *Essays*, 1955, p. 277.
[2] *Ibid.*, p. 278.
[3] *Ibid.*, p. 279.

case too the title should not be taken literally, that is as a pronouncement of Jesus' nature, but rather as a way of giving expression to his significance.[4] Such a title is a confession that the Hellenistic believers found the great eschatological redemption in Jesus.

The second important difference from Barth is that Bultmann tried to 'translate' all that the New Testament says about Jesus and his work into anthropological categories. Here we encounter the deep influence which the existentialist philosophy of the young Heidegger exerted upon him. For Bultmann all our theological knowledge is at the same time knowledge about ourselves. In an article from 1925 on the question, 'What sense does it make to speak about God?',[5] he put it thus: 'Any talk about reality which ignores the element in which alone we can have what is real, i.e., our own existence, is self-deceptive. God is never something to be seen from outside, something at our disposal, an "objective".'[6] We cannot speak of God without reference to our own concrete existential situation.[7] The same is true of our speaking of Jesus Christ. Of him, too, we cannot speak without speaking of ourselves at the same time. In this sense one can say that all theological and Christological discourse is in itself anthropological discourse. Or as W. Schmithals puts it: 'Knowledge of man is a necessary condition of the possibility of legitimate talk about God'[8] (and about Jesus Christ). This is also the way Bultmann interpreted the New Testament. Dealing with Paul's theology, he stated: 'Every assertion about God is simultaneously an assertion about man and vice versa. For this reason and in this sense Paul's theology is, at the same time, anthropology.'[9] The same is true of Paul's Christology. 'Every assertion about Christ is also an assertion about man and vice versa; and Paul's christology is simultaneously soteriology.'[10]

Bultmann summarized this whole approach in his famous 1941 lecture 'New Testament and Mythology',[11] in which he launched his programme of demythologizing. His starting-point is the conviction

---

[4] *Ibid.*, p. 280.
[5] Rudolf Bultmann, *Glauben und Verstehen* 1, 1964, pp. 26–37.
[6] *Ibid.*, p. 33.
[7] *Cf.* W. Schmithals, *An Introduction to the Theology of Rudolf Bultmann*, 1968, pp. 34f.
[8] *Ibid.*, p. 35.
[9] Rudolf Bultmann, *Theology of the New Testament* 1, 1952, p. 191.
[10] *Ibid.*, p. 191.
[11] Rudolf Bultmann, 'New Testament and Mythology', in *Kerygma and Myth* (ed. H. W. Bartsch), [5]1966, pp. 1–44.

that the New Testament is full of mythology. All the writers thought and wrote in terms of the ancient world picture. The universe is seen as a three-storeyed structure. The top department is the invisible, supernatural world of God, inhabited by angels. The lowest department is the dark underworld with its demons. In between is our human world, which is constantly influenced by the other two worlds through the intermediation of angelic and demonic powers. Yes, God himself intervenes continually in the affairs of this world and causes miraculous events to happen.

All this, however, is utterly unacceptable to modern man. We can therefore no longer accept the message of Jesus Christ as presented in the New Testament, with a literal incarnation, literal miracles, a literal atonement, a literal resurrection and a literal ascension. All these matters belong to the mythological framework of the message; the only way of discovering the message itself is to demythologize the New Testament thoroughly and radically.

But are we, in this way, not falling back into the mistakes of the older liberals? Did they not do the same? Bultmann himself believes that there is a fundamental difference. In his opinion they made a serious mistake by using the wrong method of demythologizing. Their method was one of elimination.[12] They simply cut all myths out of the Bible. The result was that Jesus turned into a moral teacher and the New Testament itself was reduced into a small booklet with some ethical precepts. His own method is quite different. It is not elimination but re-interpretation.[13] Our task is to find out what religious experiences the writers tried to express by means of all these myths. The answer to this question is not difficult. These men had discovered that in the cross of the man Jesus of Nazareth they were delivered from the power of sin.

In the same way we must also demythologize the person of Jesus. It is obvious that the New Testament gives a mythological interpretation of Jesus. It speaks of him as a pre-existent, supernatural being, who came down to earth and was born in a miraculous way. In human form he sacrificed himself for the sins of the world and died on a cross. After three days he became alive again and returned to heaven in a miraculous way. In the future he will come back from heaven to earth.

All this is pure mythology. If we want to come to a true understanding of Jesus we must again 'translate' it into anthropological,

---

[12] *Ibid.*, pp. 12f.   [13] *Ibid.*, pp. 15f.

existential categories. What the New Testament writers really wanted to do was 'to express the meaning of the historical figure of Jesus and the events of his life'.[14] What they tried to say was: 'The figure of Jesus cannot be understood simply from his inner-worldly context. In *mythological* language, this means that he stems from eternity, his origin is not a human and natural one.'[15] In *ordinary* language it means: in this man, who in himself was an ordinary man (his father and mother were well known to his contemporaries),[16] the salvation of God is present. In *theological* language it means: this man is the great eschatological event.

It is impossible here to give a thorough evaluation of Bultmann's theology. It is evident that this new approach means an enormous transformation of the biblical message. Undoubtedly, there are many biblical motifs present in Bultmann's theology, but it is also obvious that his Christology is entirely different from that of the creeds. Herman Sasse once formulated it thus: Jesus Christ was *not* conceived by the Holy Spirit, was *not* born of the *virgin* Mary; he did suffer under Pontius Pilate, was crucified, dead and buried; but he did *not* descend into hell, did *not* rise again from the dead, did *not* ascend into heaven, sits *not* at the right hand of God the Father and shall *not* come again to judge the living and the dead. All that we can say is that *somehow* in him the eschatological event of salvation took place, a fact that some time after his death was discovered by his disciples (the 'resurrection').

After Bultmann

Bultmann's theology, however, was not the end but only the beginning of a new development. The concentration on anthropological questions and on the anthropological interpretation of the Gospel soon had to give way to a new interest in the doctrine of God. Who is God after Auschwitz? Can we still speak of God's providence and of God's government of this world? What is even more, can we still speak of a personal God?

In John A. T. Robinson's *Honest to God* these questions came to the surface at a more popular level. One can put it in this way: following Paul Tillich, Robinson extended the programme of demythologizing to the Person of God himself. As modern people we can no longer think of God in terms of 'up there'. Even the change

14 *Ibid.*, p. 35.   15 *Ibid.*, p. 35.   16 *Ibid.*, p. 34.

from 'up there' to 'out there', which took place after the Copernican revolution, will no longer do, for it still means that God is seen as the One who exists above and beyond the world he made.[17] For modern man, who knows only one reality, namely this universe, there is only one way of thinking and speaking of God: not in terms of height but of depth. God is the ground of our being and of all that is; yes, he is being itself.[18]

But even this was not the end. Others went still further and propounded a God-is-dead theology. As was to be expected, this new and extreme form of theology soon withered, for the simple reason that it sawed off the branch upon which it was sitting. Yet the question that lay behind it could not be ignored. It is the question: Where do we find God in this world? Where can we find traces of his presence? This naturally led to a new concentration upon the Christological question.

The focus of the new concentration is different from that of Barth's theology.[19] To a large extent Barth's Christological concentration was a reaction against natural theology, which he saw as the *vitium originis* of both Roman Catholicism and Neo-Protestantism. Both believed that man himself can discover God in creation, history and man's own nature, by means of his own innate faculties. Barth's answer was the high Christology of the ancient church which as a faithful confession of the New Testament kerygma called a definite halt to all natural theology.

The context of the new Christological concentration is quite different. In a way it is the opposite of natural theology, namely, the atheism of modern man after Auschwitz. Modern man no longer believes in God, at least not in the God of traditional, Western theism. This God is dead indeed. But modern atheism usually goes beyond this and asserts that there are no traces whatever of (any) God in the reality of this world. But what then about Jesus Christ? The Christian church has always claimed that in him we encounter God. He is, so to speak, the 'face of God'. But is it any longer possible to maintain this?

This is the focus of the modern Christological debate: *Who is Jesus Christ really?* Is he the 'face of God'? And if so, what does this mean with regard to his person? Does it mean that he, one way or

---

[17] J. A. T. Robinson, *Honest to God*, 1963, p. 14.

[18] *Ibid.*, pp. 55ff.

[19] *Cf.* H. Berkhof, 'Hedendaagse vragen in de Christologie' (Present-day Questions in Christology), *Rondom het Woord*, November 1973, p. 1.

another, partakes of the being of God? Or is it possible to explain him in purely human categories? What really is the mystery hidden in, but also manifested by, this Jesus Christ? And what does it mean for our understanding of God and of ourselves and of this suffering world of ours?

The quest for the historical Jesus

These questions, of course, are not altogether new. Basically they are the same questions already asked in the ancient church and in the New Testament itself. The majority of present-day theologians, however, believe that we cannot simply return to the New Testament for our answers. Such a return is no longer possible for people who are aware of the implications of the various historical-critical methods that have been developed in the last two centuries. Historical-critical research has brought to light that the New Testament answers to our questions are not only human interpretations expressed in terms and concepts of that particular time, but they also appear to be of different and at times even contradictory kinds.

This approach to the New Testament actually started as early as the eighteenth century, when Lessing posthumously published the so-called 'Wolfenbüttel Fragments', parts of a large treatise written by H. S. Reimarus (1694–1768), for more than forty years professor of Hebrew and Oriental languages at Hamburg.[20] In his treatise the question who Jesus was, was approached for the first time from a historical-critical viewpoint.

Reimarus distinguished two 'systems' in the New Testament. The one is that of the Synoptic Gospels, which depicts the historical Jesus as a prophet. Jesus' own preaching was the simple message: 'Repent, for the kingdom of heaven is at hand.' Naturally this message was understood by the people as meaning that Jesus would bring in the kingdom of the Messiah and thus deliver them from the Roman yoke. But the actual course of events was quite different: Jesus died on a cross. The disciples then devised a new '*systema*' (as Reimarus calls it). Making use of Daniel's Son of man concept, they declared that the Messiah was to appear twice, once in human lowliness, the second time upon the clouds of heaven. They began to gather followers who shared their expectation of a second coming of Jesus the Messiah. At the same time they gave Jesus' death the

[20] For a summary of Reimarus' view, see A. Schweitzer, *The Quest for the Historical Jesus. A Critical Study of its Progress from Reimarus to Wrede*, 1910, pp. 13–26.

significance of a spiritual redemption and invented his resurrection. This second system we find in Paul and John, who speak of the Son of God who came down from heaven, suffered and died, but arose again and ascended to heaven. Reimarus himself accepted the first system as the true picture and regarded the second as an aberration from the first, leading to a deification of the historical Jesus.

Since Reimarus this problem has been at the centre of all Christological discussions and the answer has sharply divided the theologians.[21] In the nineteenth century, for instance, there were, broadly speaking, two main schools of thought. The *orthodox* school refused to accept a division between two 'systems' in the New Testament. They pointed out that in the New Testament itself the so-called second system is older than the first. Paul's letters are much older than the Gospels. What is more, Paul himself appealed to still older layers of tradition (*cf.* 1 Cor. 15:1–3). The orthodox school therefore believed that it had to adhere to the decision of Chalcedon: Jesus is true God and true man in the unity of the divine person of the Son. The *liberal* school of thought followed the road shown by Reimarus and took its starting-point in the so-called historical Jesus. The result was a Jesus who was at most a prophet, showing us in word and deed who God is: the loving Father of all mankind. The 'fine flower of this enterprise'[22] and the classical expression of this liberal view is to be found in Adolf von Harnack's *What is Christianity?*[23] In his eighth lecture he condenses it all into one sentence: 'The Gospel, as Jesus proclaimed it, has to do with the Father only, not with the Son.'[24] In other words, the parable of the prodigal son is the summary of the gospel: all that has to happen is the return of the son to the waiting Father who loves him.

We cannot pursue the older quest any further. Suffice it to say that just as the quest had seemingly attained its goal, it took an embarrassing turn.[25] Using the very same historical-critical method to the full, Wrede, Wellhausen and, a little later, the form critics showed that the picture drawn by the older liberal school was not a scientific picture at all. In his famous book *The Quest of the Historical Jesus*, Albert Schweitzer gave a vivid description of the old quest, but at the same time wrote its obituary.

---

[21] *Cf.* H. Berkhof, *art. cit.*, p. 2. I am greatly indebted to this article in which Berkhof gives a summary of recent developments.
[22] R. H. Fuller, *The New Testament in Current Study*, 1962, pp. 26f.
[23] Original German title: *Das Wesen des Christentums*, 1900; E.T. 1901.
[24] *Ibid.*, p. 147. [25] *Cf.* R. H. Fuller, *op. cit.*, pp. 27f.

The new quest for the historical Jesus

Nevertheless, when in the fifties of this century Christology again became the centre of discussion, all the old questions returned, especially the question of the historical Jesus. In Barth's theology this question had not played any part. Barth read the New Testament from the vantage-point of Pauline and Johannine theology. In the Gospels, too, he found the story of the Son of God who became flesh.

The question had also been avoided by Bultmann, but for quite a different reason. At first glance Bultmann seemed to be on the same track as Barth, for he too took his starting-point in the 'kerygmatic' Christ as preached by Paul and John. In actual fact, however, there was a profound difference between Bultmann and Barth. Bultmann, one of the fathers of New Testament Form and Tradition Criticism, believed that it is impossible to discover the historical Jesus. In his small book *Jesus and the Word*[26] he frankly stated: 'We can, strictly speaking, know nothing of the personality of Jesus.'[27] At a later stage he did admit that we can know a few facts, but this does not help us much. We do not know, for example, how Jesus interpreted his own death. All we know is that Jesus was executed by the Romans as a political criminal.[28]

But this lack of knowledge does not really matter, for according to Bultmann the historical Jesus himself does not constitute the kerygma. The real content of the message is the crucified Jesus. In his cross the cosmological-eschatological redemption took place. The disciples discovered this on the day of Easter. All of a sudden (how, we do not know[29]) they realized that the cross is the final saving event, and immediately they began to preach this message. The really important thing for us is this preached message, this *kerygma*. 'Through the word of preaching the cross and the resurrection are made present: the eschatological "now" is here, and the promise of Is. 49:8 is fulfilled: "Behold, now is the acceptable time; behold, now is the day of salvation".'[30]

It was to be expected that this 'escape' into the 'kerygmatic Christ' by Bultmann would evoke a reaction. Does the New Testament

[26] First German edition in 1926; E.T. 1935.
[27] *Ibid.*, p. 9.   [28] R. H. Fuller, *op. cit.*, p. 49.
[29] There is a great deal of ambiguity in Bultmann's views at this very point. *Cf.* G. E. Ladd, *The New Testament and Criticism*, 1967, p. 188.
[30] In 'New Testament and Mythology', *Kerygma and Myth*, pp. 42f.

really allow us to ignore the historical Jesus completely and concentrate one-sidedly on the Christ of faith? In 1954 one of Bultmann's own students, Ernst Käsemann, wrote an article on 'The Problem of the Historical Jesus',[31] in which he accused his teacher of docetism! Käsemann and the other neo-Bultmannians took their starting-point again in the historical Jesus himself, for, so they maintained, the historical Jesus is the foundation for the message about the Christ of faith.[32] Although it may be true that we cannot accept the Gospels at face value, because they are overlaid with the many layers of the post-Easter tradition, nevertheless it is possible to dig through the post-Easter witness and arrive at a pre-Easter stratum. In this stratum we can discover 'Jesus' own implicit christological self-understanding'.[33]

Nearly all the post-Bultmannians tried to put this self-understanding of Jesus into one comprehensive formula. G. Ebeling spoke of Jesus' faith, E. Fuchs of his attitude or conduct (German: *Verhalten*), Paul Van Buren of his freedom. But whatever term they used, they all believed that this unique self-understanding of Jesus was the basis for the later apostolic Christ-kerygma. At the same time they also believed that the Christ-kerygma is not a simple continuation of the implicit Christology, hidden in the self-understanding of the historical Jesus. The kerygma about the Christ of faith is something altogether new compared with the preaching of Jesus himself. The great change is that the Proclaimer has become the Proclaimed. Jesus with his faith now has become the object of faith, and the secret of this transformation is the resurrection.[34]

All post-Bultmannians, both those belonging to the right wing and those belonging to the left wing, put much emphasis on the resurrection. At the same time they were all extremely vague about its historicity. In most cases one gets the impression that the resurrection is the work of the interpreting Christian congregation rather than an act of God in the life of Jesus himself. No wonder that in

[31] Original publication in *Zeitschrift für Theologie und Kirche*, 51 (1954), pp. 125ff. E.T. in *Essays on New Testament Themes* (tr. W. J. Montague), 1964, pp. 15–47.

[32] For a summary of the New Quest, see R. H. Fuller, *op. cit.*, pp. 25–53. The *TSF Bulletin* of Autumn 1966 (no. 46) is wholly devoted to the theme: 'The Jesus of History and the Christ of Faith'. At the end of his article R. E. Nixon gives a short bibliography of most important work available in English up to 1966. *Op. cit.*, pp. 15f.

[33] R. H. Fuller, *op. cit.*, p. 42.

[34] *Cf.* G. Ebeling, *The Nature of Faith*, 1961, pp. 58–71.

the early sixties the debate concentrated on the resurrection.[35]

In spite of all the strictures one can pass on the new quest for the historical Jesus, it cannot be denied that this new quest was a great improvement compared with the view of Bultmann himself. It dealt with a real problem: What is the connection between the earthly Jesus before the resurrection and the Christ proclaimed by the apostolic church? Gradually it has become clear that the two cannot really be separated. They belong together. Or better still, they are the one Jesus Christ. Undoubtedly, there is an element of discontinuity, but it is embedded in an essential continuity. R. H. Fuller's formulation is apt: 'The pre-Good Friday historical Jesus proclaimed that in himself God was beginning his eschatological action and was about to consummate that action. The post-Easter kerygma proclaims that in Jesus' life, death and resurrection God *has* (note the difference of tenses) acted eschatologically, although that action still has to be rounded off in the future.'[36] And how do we know this? Because God raised him from the dead. The resurrection of Jesus is not only the decisive turning-point in his own life, but it is also the decisive framework of reference, within and by which we can understand who Jesus is and what he did.

Still, the new quest, however much an improvement on Bultmann, could not really proceed beyond the rather vague notion that the Christ of faith is 'the Jesus of Nazareth in whom, according to the kerygma and to faith, God has acted decisively for man's redemption'.[37] The question still remained open: But who is he? Is he what the New Testament proclaims him to be: the Son of God? Is he what the ancient creeds profess him to be: *vere Deus* and *vere homo*? These questions were bound to come back.

In fact, they soon did come back. From the mid-sixties onward a great number of new Christological concepts have been published. Very broadly speaking, they can be divided into two groups. First, there are some important studies which, being in the Barthian tradition, want to go beyond and improve upon the decision of Chalcedon by trying to overcome some of the seemingly inherent

---

[35] *Cf.* the following literature (which is only a selection): Daniel P. Fuller, *Easter Faith and History*, 1965; B. Klappert (ed.), *Diskussion um Kreuz und Auferstehung*, 1967; C. F. D. Moule (ed.), *The Significance of the Message of the Resurrection for Faith in Jesus Christ*, 1968; Willy Marxsen, *The Resurrection of Jesus of Nazareth*, 1970.

[36] R. H. Fuller, *op. cit.*, p. 140.   [37] *Ibid.*, p. 142.

31

weaknesses of the ancient Christology. The second group of studies abandons Chalcedon altogether, because the authors believe that it does no justice to the person of Jesus as depicted in the New Testament Gospels. Taking their starting-point in the historical Jesus, they try to offer a Christology that is faithful to both the New Testament data and the modes of thought of contemporary man.

Chapter Four

Beyond Chalcedon: Wolfhart Pannenberg and Jürgen Moltmann

Wolfhart Pannenberg

One of the first to tackle these questions in a new way was Wolfhart Pannenberg in his major work *Jesus: God and man*.[1] He believes that a new approach is necessary. First, we must go behind the straightforward incarnational approach which has been characteristic of traditional Christology.[2] Secondly, we must take into account that we live after the Enlightenment and that since then a growing cleft has emerged between the historical picture of Jesus on the one hand, and dogmatic Christology on the other.[3] The latter does not mean that we have to make a simple choice. As a matter of fact, Pannenberg believes that we have to take seriously both history and the dogmatic tradition. If we neglect the tradition, we shall arrive only at 'generalizations of certain aspects of his [Jesus'] appearance that are astonishingly superficial and hasty'.[4] Yet the two factors mentioned do mean that methodologically we have to prefer a Christology 'from below' to a Christology 'from above'.[5]

The approach 'from above' is that of traditional Christology. One finds it in the ancient Christologies (Ignatius, the Apologists, Athanasius), those of the Reformation (although in the case of Luther there are also other lines of thought), and those of Barth and Brunner. Common to them all is that they start with the doctrine of the Trinity and then go on to ask how the Second Person of the Trinity (the Logos) assumed a human nature.

Pannenberg objects to this for three weighty reasons: (i) such an approach presupposes the divinity of Jesus; (ii) it makes it difficult to recognize the distinctive features of the real historical man, Jesus of Nazareth; (iii) it virtually adopts the position of God himself by

[1] E.T. 1968. Original German title: *Grundzüge der Christologie*, 1964.
[2] *Ibid.*, p. 11.   [3] *Ibid.*, p. 11.
[4] *Ibid.*, p. 12.   [5] *Ibid.*, p. 33.

concentrating upon the way God's Son came into the world.[6] This rejection of the approach 'from above' does not mean that Pannenberg rejects the idea of incarnation altogether and that he regards the incarnational Christology as a total mistake. In fact, he himself also accepts the concept of incarnation; but he sees it as the mistake of traditional Christology that it took this concept as a starting-point rather than as a *goal* of Christology.[7]

Pannenberg himself also believes that Jesus is the Son of God. In another article he writes that the central affirmation of the Christian church is 'that in dealing with Jesus we are dealing with God himself'.[8] But he believes that in order to discover this we must start 'from below', *i.e.*, with the historical Jesus, for the Christian community's confession of Christ is grounded in the activity and fate of the man Jesus. But can we really know this activity and fate of the man Jesus? Over against Bultmann and in agreement with the post-Bultmannians Pannenberg maintains that we indeed can go back behind the apostolic kerygma to the historical Jesus.[9]

It is clear from the Gospels that Jesus' immediate context was that of Jewish apocalyptic expectation.[10] Jesus expected the absolute end of history, with the general resurrection of the dead, the appearance of the heavenly Son of man, and the beginning of the Last Judgment. Within this framework Jesus fulfilled his office to call men into the kingdom of God which had appeared in him.[11] 'He was certain that in his activity the future salvation of God's Kingdom had broken into the present time.'[12] It is evident, of course, that in issuing this call Jesus made a tremendous claim of authority. He claimed no less than to speak with the authority of God.

At the same time this claim had a *proleptic* structure: it needed future vindication by God himself. Jesus' expectation of this vindication, however, seemed to become one great failure, for by the leaders of his own people he was condemned as a blasphemer, and subsequently he was executed as a rebel by the Romans. He died on a cross. But three days later the great miracle happened: God raised

---

[6] *Ibid.*, pp. 34, 35. *Cf.* also p. 301 and his critique of Barth's position on p. 313.

[7] *Ibid.*, p. 301. *Cf.* also the quotation from Althaus on p. 29.

[8] In James Robinson and John B. Cobb Jr (eds.), *Theology and History, New Frontiers in Theology* 3, 1967, p. 101. *Cf.* also *Jesus: God and man*, p. 21 and *passim*.

[9] *Ibid.*, p. 24.

[10] *Ibid.*, pp. 61ff.

[11] *Ibid.*, p. 212.

[12] *Ibid.*, p. 217.

him from the dead and thus vindicated him and his claim.[13] True, the final end of history did not yet come, but Jesus' resurrection can mean nothing else than the proleptic anticipation of this end.[14]

At the same time it also became manifest who Jesus really is. In the resurrection, the Christology 'from below' issues in an eschatological Christology, in which it becomes clear that 'as *this* man, as man in this particular, unique situation, with this particular historical mission and this particular fate – as this man, Jesus is not just man, but from the perspective of his resurrection from the dead . . . he is one with God and is himself God'.[15]

But is this not in conflict with what we read about the historical Jesus who regarded himself as entirely subordinate to the Father? Pannenberg's answer is: exactly this subordination is in retrospect the expression of Jesus' essential unity as Son with the Father. As the One wholly dedicated to the Father Jesus is the Revealer of God's divinity and belongs inseparably to God's essence. Thus already in his pre-Easter life Jesus was the Son of God, although he was not yet recognizable as such. Yes, the legend of the virgin birth[16] affirms that he was the Son of God from the beginning. What is even more, we must speak of his pre-existence.[17] God was always one with Jesus, even prior to his earthly birth. Ultimately we can speak of Jesus only in terms of incarnation. The concept of incarnation, even though we cannot take it as our starting-point in the Christology, nevertheless affirms a truth that cannot be abandoned.[18] 'In Jesus, God himself has come out of his otherness into our world, into human form, and in such a way that the Father-Son relation that – as we know in retrospect – always belonged to God's essence now acquired corporeal form.'[19]

This is not in contradiction with the fact that Jesus always distinguished himself from God, whom he called his Father. On the contrary, Pannenberg asserts that 'the distinction that Jesus main-

---

[13] *Ibid.*, pp. 67, 135. For a discussion of Jesus' resurrection as a historical problem, see *Ibid.*, pp. 88–106. *Cf.* also E. Frank Tupper, *The Theology of Wolfhart Pannenberg*, 1973, pp. 151–160 (Pannenberg's own view) and pp. 274–285 (a discussion of Pannenberg's critics), and also Don H. Olive, *Wolfhart Pannenberg* (in the series: *Makers of the Modern Theological Mind*), 1973, pp. 56–64.

[14] *Ibid.*, p. 68. *Cf.* pp. 106–108 on the delay of the Parousia.

[15] *Ibid.*, p. 323; *cf.* also p. 69: 'If Jesus, having been raised from the dead, is ascended to God and if thereby the end of the world has begun, then God is ultimately revealed in Jesus'.

[16] *Cf. Ibid.*, pp. 141–150. [17] *Cf. Ibid.*, pp. 150–155.

[18] *Cf. Ibid.*, p. 155. [19] *Ibid.*, p. 156; *cf.* p. 322.

tained between himself and the Father also belongs to the Trinity of God'.[20] Thus Pannenberg's Christology 'from below' issues in a fully-fledged doctrine of the Trinity,[21] which he expresses with the help of the Hegelian concept of personality.[22]

But does this not mean that again the humanity of Jesus, the *vere homo*, is swallowed up by the *vere Deus*? In his answer to this question Pannenberg actually falls back upon the sixth-century doctrine of the *anhypostasis* and *enhypostasis*. But he hastens to explain that this does not mean a partition of Jesus into two natures. In fact, he is rather critical of the term 'nature'. He prefers to speak of two 'complementary aspects'. He states: 'The humanity of the man Jesus is not synthesized with a divine essence, but it involves two complementary total aspects of his existence. These aspects are as different from one another as God and man are different.'[23] But a little further on in the same paragraph he writes: 'The divine Sonship designates the root in which Jesus' human existence, connected with the Father and nevertheless distinguished from him, has the ground of its unity and of its meaning.'[24] And five pages later he expresses it even more clearly: 'Precisely as this man, Jesus is the Son of God and thus himself God. . . . He is not to be thought of as a synthesis of the divine and the human. . . . Precisely *in* his particular humanity Jesus is the Son of God. Thereby . . . his divine Sonship constitutes the particularity of this man.'[25] Actually, this is nothing but the ancient doctrine of *anhypostasis* and *enhypostasis* in modern words.

Evaluation

It is evident that Pannenberg's Christology, though starting 'from below' (*i.e.* from the historical Jesus), through the turning-point of the resurrection, ultimately comes very close to the classical Christology. It may be true that he does not want to speak of two 'natures'[26] and prefers to speak of the 'indirect identity' of 'two complementary total aspects of Jesus' existence', but this does not alter the fact that basically his view is a variant of the Chalcedonian

---

[20] *Ibid.*, p. 159.
[21] 'If Father, Son, and Spirit are distinct but coordinate moments in the accomplishment of God's revelation, then they are so in God's eternal essence as well', *Ibid.*, p. 180.
[22] *Cf. Ibid.*, pp. 181f., 336.   [23] *Ibid.*, p. 337; *cf.* pp. 95, 155.
[24] *Ibid.*, p. 337.   [25] *Ibid.*, p. 342.
[26] *Cf.* his critique of Chalcedon, *Ibid.*, p. 284.

tradition.[27] In spite of his critique of Barth, he essentially shares Barth's thinking in categories of revelation. Emphatically he declares: 'What belongs to God's revelation also belongs to the essence of God, if the revelation reveals God himself.'[28] Perhaps Pannenberg is even more consistent at this very point than Barth. He does not hesitate to see essential elements in the attitude of the man Jesus, such as humility, obedience, subordination, yes, even his ignorance, as belonging to the very essence of God.

An important aspect of Pannenberg's Christology, as we have seen, is his decision to develop a Christology 'from below'. We believe that such an approach has definite merits. For one thing, it takes the historicity of Jesus seriously. For another, it takes his resurrection seriously as the great turning-point in Jesus' life and work.

At the same time we cannot overlook the fact that Pannenberg adopts a rather critical attitude to the biblical data about Jesus and often uses the historical-critical method to get rid of conflicting evidence. Thus the virgin birth, which does not fit in too well with his approach 'from below', is labelled a 'legend'.[29] Likewise the self-consciousness of Jesus as the Messiah and the Son of God, which in the Gospels is attributed to Jesus, is denied, because 'today it must be taken as all but certain that the pre-Easter Jesus neither designated himself as Messiah (or Son of God) nor accepted such a confession to him from others'.[30] The latter point is the more remarkable, because in our opinion it is not necessarily demanded by the approach 'from below'. As a matter of fact, it could fit in very well with a Christology that starts with the historical Jesus. Within Pannenberg's own framework it could well be a part of Jesus' claim that also had to be validated by the resurrection.

Personally I have no fundamental objection to a Christological concept that starts 'from below'. I believe that it brings out aspects of Jesus' person and work that are easily overlooked in a Christology 'from above'. Moreover, it is the very same way along which the apostolic church came to its confession of Jesus as Messiah, as Lord, as the Son of God. At the same time, however, I believe that we who are living after Paul and John have to complement a Christology 'from below' by a Christology 'from above'. We who know Jesus

[27] Thus H. Berkhof, 'Schoonenberg en Pannenberg: de tweesprong van de huidige christologie', *Tijdschrift voor Theologie* 11 (1974), p. 419.
[28] W. Pannenberg, *op. cit.*, p. 175.   [29] *Ibid.*, pp. 143, 150, 358, 361.
[30] *Ibid.*, p. 327.

as the risen One also have to go the way from the *vere Deus* to the *vere homo*. Pannenberg calls the concept of incarnation God's way of looking at Jesus.[31] This may be so, but for us who know that by the resurrection Jesus has been designated Son of God in power (Rom. 1:4) is it not a perfectly legitimate way of looking at the mystery of Jesus Christ? Now that God has revealed his way of looking at Jesus to us, may we not, indeed must we not, also use this approach in order to get a 'complete' picture of Jesus who is at the same time *vere Deus* and *vere homo*?

Finally, Pannenberg's insistence in the Christology 'from below' may also be the reason why he ultimately comes to an eschatological *enhypostasis* of all men. In Jesus the essence of God and the essence of man are integrated. This happened in the particularity of Jesus' historical life, Pannenberg says, but then he immediately adds that in the future this integration will extend to all human reality.[32] One wonders whether in this way the Christology 'from below' does not issue in a deification of man.

Jürgen Moltmann

A similar line of thought, but leading to far greater consequences for the doctrine of God, is found in two other post-Barthian Christological projects, namely, those of Jürgen Moltmann and Eberhard Jüngel. In 1972 Moltmann published his second programmatic work under the title *Der gekreuzigte Gott*.[33] Five years later Jüngel published his major work *Gott als Geheimnis der Welt. Zur Begründung der Theologie des Gekreuzigten im Streit zwischen Theismus und Atheismus*.[34] Both books were written against the background of the 'a-theism' of the God-is-dead theology and are an attempt to develop a new 'theo'-logy based on a new understanding of Jesus Christ.

There are, of course, important differences. Yet both books show a significant similarity in approach and their conclusions, too, show a great deal of similarity. In this chapter we shall concentrate on Moltmann, whose book has created a great deal of interest in the English-speaking world.

In the introduction to his book, called 'In explanation of the theme', Moltmann tells us that his interest in a 'theology of the

---

[31] *Ibid.*, p. 35.   [32] *Ibid.*, p. 344.   [33] E.T. *The Crucified God*, 1974.
[34] E.T. *God as the Mystery of the World: On the Foundation of the Theology of the Crucified One in the Dispute between Theism and Atheism*, 1983.

cross' (a *theologia crucis*) goes back to the years immediately following World War 2, when he and the other survivors of his generation
were returning from camps and hospitals to the lecture room. In
that situation 'a theology which did not speak of God in the sight
of the one who was abandoned and crucified would have had nothing
to say to us'.[35]

He also points out that he is not the first theologian to develop a
theology of the cross. He mentions, among others, Paul and Luther,
the early dialectical theology and the Luther renaissance of the
1920s.[36] In all the earlier concepts, however, the main emphasis was
always on the context of personal salvation. Moltmann himself wants
to go beyond this and, therefore, he not only asks: 'Who is God in
the cross of the Christ who was abandoned by God?', but also:
'What does this mean for the liberation of man in general?' Hence
the book consists of three main parts: the Christology, the doctrine
of God (especially the Trinitarian being of God) and the liberation
of man. There can be no doubt that the main purpose of the book
is found in the last part. The new Christology of the cross and the
new *theologia crucis* are developed in order to give an answer to the
desperate cries of a suffering and dying humanity.

The fundamental starting-point of Moltmann is found in the following statement: 'God is revealed in the cross of Christ who was
abandoned by God. . . . The epistemological principle of the theology of the cross can only be this dialectical principle: the deity of
God is revealed in the paradox of the cross.'[37] In taking this
starting-point he takes up again and radicalizes Luther's statement
that God can only be known *sub contrario* (in the guise of the
opposite).[38] I call it a radicalization, because Moltmann develops it
into a dialectical principle[39] that governs his whole theology and
leads to a new Christian praxis of liberation.

But what is the meaning of the *cross* for Moltmann? In answering
this question he uses a twofold approach. The first (in chapter 4) is
of a 'historical' nature. He asks: What is left of Jesus' claim to be
the coming One in the face of his crucifixion? We have to take this
crucifixion utterly seriously. Jesus died there as the One rejected by
the Father. 'The cross of the Son divides God from God to the
utmost degree of enmity and distinction.'[40]

The second approach (in chapter 5), which he calls 'eschatological',

---

[35] *The Crucified God*, p. 1.   [36] *Ibid.*, p. 3.   [37] *Ibid.*, p. 27.
[38] *Cf.* P. Althaus, *The Theology of Martin Luther*, 1966, pp. 25ff.
[39] J. Moltmann, *op. cit.*, p. 27.   [40] *Ibid.*, p. 152.

is as it were a movement backwards. Now he asks: How is it possible that he who was raised from the dead and who is proclaimed as the risen One had to die on a cross, and why is 'the word of the cross' still constitutive for the Christian proclamation? The New Testament replies: Because there he died 'for us'. This 'for us' should not simply be interpreted as 'for our sins', although it must be admitted that this too is being said in the New Testament. Yet such a 'theory of expiatory sacrifice' is only a 'secondary interpretation of the fundamental "for us" '.[41] The real meaning of the 'for us' is much wider and much deeper. It is that the God who raised Jesus is the God who crucified him! And this can only mean that we must 'seek to understand God in the passion, in the crucifixion of Jesus'.[42]

Moltmann is well aware of the fact that he is not the first one to relate God to the passion and cross of Christ. He mentions the names of several other theologians, including Karl Rahner and in particular Karl Barth, with his Christological concentration of all theology. In fact, he is very appreciative of Barth's view. 'Barth has consistently drawn the harshness of the cross into his concept of God.' 'Because Barth thought consistently of "God in Christ", he could think historically of God's being, speak almost in theopaschite terms of God's suffering and being involved in the cross of the Son.'[43] Yet Barth did not go far enough. Although he did apply the cross to God, he applied it only to a 'simple' concept of God. In other words, his approach was not sufficiently Trinitarian. 'When one considers the significance of the death of Jesus for God himself, one must enter into the inter-trinitarian tensions and relationships of God and speak of the Father, the Son and the Spirit.'[44] The cross is not just something that happened to the man Jesus, but it happened to God himself. 'The Christ event on the cross is a God event',[45] and therefore the cross is the self-revelation of God as the triune God. 'What happens on the cross manifests the relationships of Jesus, the Son, to the Father, and vice versa.' At the same time 'the cross and its liberating effect makes possible the movement of the Spirit from the Father to us'.[46]

Does speaking of the cross as 'a God event' mean that we really must speak of the death of God on the cross? In other words, is this theology of the cross no more than another form of the so-called

---

[41] *Ibid.*, p. 187.   [42] *Ibid.*, p. 190.   [43] *Ibid.*, p. 203.
[44] *Ibid.*, p. 204.   [45] *Ibid.*, p. 205.
[46] *Ibid.*, pp. 206f.; *cf.* also pp. 238–240, 243–246.

death-of-God theology? To be sure, Moltmann more than once uses such expressions as the death of God[47] and the crucified God.[48]

But such expressions have to be seen within the Trinitarian framework that he has accepted. This framework enables him to speak of the death of God with reference to Christ's death without implying the death of the Father. In fact, he rejects the idea of 'patripassianism', *i.e.*, the view of the modalists who denied the ontological Trinity and therefore maintained that actually the Father suffered (and died) in his manifestation as Son.

At the same time Moltmann upholds the idea of 'patri*com*passianism',[49] *i.e.*, the Father suffered *with* the Son. Paul expressed this when he wrote that 'God did not spare his own Son, but gave him up for us all' (Rom. 8:32). In his exposition of this 'giving up' Moltmann quotes W. Popkes: 'We must understand "deliver up" in its full sense and not water it down to mean "send" or "give". What happened here is what Abraham did not need to do to Isaac; Christ was quite deliberately abandoned by the Father to the fate of death; God subjected him to the power of corruption, whether this be called man or death . . . God made Christ sin (II Cor. 5:21), Christ is the accursed of God. A theology of the cross cannot be expressed more radically than it is here.'[50] There is therefore only one conclusion possible: 'In the passion of the Son, the Father himself suffers the pains of abandonment. In the death of the Son, death comes upon God himself, and the Father suffers the death of his Son in his love for forsaken man.'[51]

It is evident that here Moltmann balances on the tightrope of pure theopaschitism, even of patripassianism. In the same context he does not hesitate to say that 'God himself died in Jesus for us'.[52] Yet a little later he emphatically states that theopaschitic talk of the death of God, 'on closer inspection, . . . will not hold'.[53] Actually we should not speak of the death of Jesus as the death *of* God, but rather as death *in* God.[54] In the death of Jesus on the cross God has taken up suffering and death into his own being. This should not be limited to Jesus' own suffering and death, for Jesus was not just an individual but the representative man.[55] Therefore, in the death of

---

[47] Cf. *Ibid.*, p. 192.   [48] Cf. *Ibid.*, pp. 190, 192, 195f.
[49] Cf. Jürgen Moltmann, 'Gesichtspunkte der Kreuzestheologie heute', *Evangelische Theologie*, 1973/74, p. 359.
[50] *The Crucified God*, p. 191.
[51] *Ibid.*, p. 192.   [52] *Ibid.*, p. 192.   [53] *Ibid.*, p. 203.
[54] *Ibid.*, p. 207.   [55] Cf. *Ibid.*, p. 183.

Jesus on the cross God has taken up all the suffering of this world into himself. 'All human history, however much it may be determined by guilt and death, is taken up into this "history of God", i.e., into the Trinity, and integrated into the future of the "history of God". There is no suffering which in this history of God is not God's suffering; no death which has not been God's death in the history of Golgotha.'[56]

How seriously this is meant by Moltmann appears from the fact that in this context he emphatically mentions Auschwitz. Even Auschwitz is taken up into God and integrated into his history.[57] The 'bifurcation' in God contains the whole uproar of history within itself.[58] And this means true salvation, for if all human history, with all its suffering, guilt and death, is taken up into this 'history of God', it is also taken up into the future of the history of God, i.e., the victory of God over suffering, guilt and death.[59]

Evaluation

It is no wonder that Moltmann's book (and the same is true of Jüngel's book that, in spite of its difficult theological and philosophical language, has already gone through several German editions) has made such an impact. In a world that in misery and despair cries out for a ray of hope, this book seems to take the reality of suffering and death utterly seriously. It does this by relating both this reality of suffering and death to the cross of Jesus Christ, and the cross itself to the very heart of God's being. The cross is not something that affects God only partially (namely, God as Son) and temporarily (Good Friday), but the cross is 'the history of God' himself. In the cross God takes all suffering and all death up into his own history and therefore into his own being. Who is God? In sum, the answer to that question can be found only on the cross: He is 'the crucified God'.

At this very point, however, our questions also start.

---

[56] Ibid., p. 246. Jüngel's emphasis is slightly different. He prefers to speak of transitoriness (Vergänglichkeit) and nothingness (das Nichts), to which God exposes himself, op. cit., pp. 292ff. In the death of Christ on the cross God has integrated nothingness into his own life and history and thus triumphed over it, op. cit., pp. 296ff.

[57] Cf. The Crucified God, pp. 267–278.   [58] Ibid., p. 246.

[59] In his later work, The Trinity and the Kingdom of God (German ed. 1980), Moltmann consistently speaks of 'God's self-redemption from the suffering of his love' (pp. 75f.).

1. Is the idea of the 'crucified God' really scriptural? We do realize that Moltmann in using such a term opposes the metaphysical concept of God which has been very common in the Christian tradition. Rightly he does away with the whole idea of an apathetic God who cannot really be involved in the suffering of this world and who was not really involved in the suffering of Christ either. Here he is in line with Luther who also maintained 'that the deity of Christ, because of the incarnation and of its personal unity with humanity, enters into the uttermost depths of its suffering'. Luther therefore did not hesitate to say that 'God suffers in Christ'.[60] But can we go beyond this? Luther always refused to do this. To him the suffering of God was an incomprehensible mystery which even the angels cannot fully understand.

I believe that Luther was right here. It is striking that such expressions as 'the crucified God' and 'the death of God' are entirely absent from Scripture. This is the more striking because the New Testament writers evidently believed that Jesus was the Son of God in the ontological sense of the word. Yet they were apparently of the opinion that all such expressions had to be avoided. When they speak of the crucified One they always speak of him as the *Son* of God, never as *God*. Furthermore, they always speak of him as the Son of God *in his human existence*. It is the Son as he became man, who was crucified and raised from the dead. When he is forsaken by God, he does not cry: 'My Father, my Father, why hast thou forsaken me?', but he cries: 'My God, my God, why hast thou forsaken me?' It is the man Jesus, hanging on the cross as our representative, who is forsaken by his God. Undoubtedly this also raises questions as to the inter-trinitarian relationship between Father and Son, but it is certainly quite different from Moltmann's interpretation of the cross as an event within God himself. In my opinion Moltmann here goes beyond the restrained language of Scripture, and the resulting 'theology of the cross' is a speculative construction that at crucial points shows more affinity to Hegel than to the biblical kerygma.[61]

2. Our second question is whether Moltmann's almost exclusive concentration on the cross is not at the expense of the resurrection. Admittedly, he does not deny the resurrection. In fact in his first major work, *Theology of Hope*,[62] the focus was very much on the

[60] P. Althaus, *op. cit.*, p. 197.
[61] *Cf.* the many references to Hegel in his book, especially p. 246.
[62] Published in 1964. E.T. 1967.

resurrection (while the cross played only a minor role). Now it is just the opposite. But is this really possible? Can we, theologically, speak of the cross without speaking at the same time of the resurrection? It is striking indeed that the same Paul, who summarizes his whole message in the expression 'the word of the cross' (1 Cor. 1:18; cf. 2:2), never speaks of God as the One who suffered with Jesus on the cross, but again and again as the God who raised Jesus from the dead (cf. Rom. 4:24; 8:11; Gal. 1:1; 2 Cor. 4:14; Col. 2:12; 1 Thes. 1:10). The resurrection is not only the manifestation of the hidden meaning of the cross, but it is the next stage in the history of salvation, revealing God as the One who conquers sin, suffering and death by raising his Son from the dead and establishing him as Lord. For this very reason Barth based the doctrine of the Trinity not on the cross but on the resurrection. 'The doctrine of the Trinity is nothing else than the unfolding of the knowledge that Jesus is the Christ or the Lord.'[63]

3. Can one really speak of death *in* God? Again we note that the Bible, which often speaks of God and death in one and the same context, explicitly avoids this kind of language. Nowhere do we find even a trace of the idea that God takes up death into himself, into his own being. According to the unanimous testimony of Scripture, death is the enemy, which is *destroyed* by God: first and principally in the resurrection of Jesus Christ (cf. 2 Tim. 1:10), finally and definitely in the resurrection of all God's children (cf. 1 Cor. 15:26).

4. A similar question arises when Moltmann speaks of the inclusion of *all* human suffering and death into the history of God. Is this view not Hegelian rather than scriptural? Several critics have pointed out that Moltmann, in spite of his deep concern for the suffering of this world, in actual fact does not take this suffering seriously enough. In his dialectical telescoping of the whole history of suffering and death into the 'history of God', he at least gives the impression that suffering and death are a necessary part of the history of God and that the history of the world *is* the history of God, which from thesis through antithesis moves on to a new synthesis. But on this view are not both the suffering of Jesus on the cross and the suffering of man in this world of bloodshed robbed of their very concreteness and harshness? To start with the latter, the suffering of man is too real, too cruel, too incomprehensible to be 'explained' by a dialectical inclusion of all suffering into the being of God. As

---

[63] Karl Barth, *CD* I, 1, p. 384.

H. H. Miskotte puts it: 'Suffering in general, opaque and absurd as it is, is an open question to God.'[64] But the suffering of Christ on the cross cannot be 'explained' either as a purely inter-trinitarian event. Miskotte continues: 'The suffering of the Son is God's open question to man, the creator of Auschwitz and all inhumanity. He asks whether we are willing to acknowledge his just judgment on us, which He executed once and for all on Golgotha.'

5. Next, Moltmann's view, just as that of Pannenberg, seems to lead to an eschatological and universalistic divinization of man. 'Man is taken up, without limitations and conditions, into the life, the death and resurrection of God, and in faith participates corporeally in the fullness of God. There is nothing that can exclude him from the situation of God between the grief of the Father, the love of the Son and the drive of the Spirit. . . . The human God who encounters man in the crucified Christ thus involves man in a realistic divinization (*theosis*).'[65] Again one cannot help wondering whether this is not in line with the Hegelian rather than the biblical eschatology.

6. Finally, there is the question: What is left of Chalcedon? To be honest, this question is very hard to answer. On the one hand, Moltmann certainly agrees with Chalcedon that Jesus is both *vere Deus* and *vere homo*. On the other hand, the doctrine of the two natures does not really play a part in his book. In fact, he more than once warns against the interpretation of Jesus' death on the cross in terms of the relationship between the divine and the human nature of Christ, because in such a view the event of the cross is understood statically 'as a reciprocal relationship between two qualitatively different natures, the divine nature which is incapable of suffering and the human nature which is capable of suffering'.[66] We must begin from the totality of the person of Christ and understand the relationship of the death of the Son to the Father and the Spirit. The question that cannot be avoided here is whether in this conception the humanity of Jesus is still taken seriously. The cross is first of all an event in God, a Trinitarian event that manifests the relationships of Jesus the Son, and the Father and the Spirit.[67] But in this way, what is left of the central biblical idea that Jesus acts as the representative of mankind in relation to God? What is left of what Paul

[64] H. H. Miskotte in *Diskussion über Jürgen Moltmanns Buch 'Der Gekreuzigte Gott'* (ed. M. Welker), 1979, pp. 92.
[65] *The Crucified God*, p. 277.
[66] *Ibid.*, p. 245; cf. pp. 205f.
[67] *Ibid.*, p. 206.

writes to Timothy: 'There is one mediator between God and men, the *man* Christ Jesus'? For the fathers of Chalcedon it was just as necessary to maintain the *vere homo* as the *vere Deus*. Hence they stressed the *homoousion* (of the same substance) equally with regard to the humanity as to the deity. In the conception of Moltmann the former seems to recede into the background in favour of the latter.

Chapter Five

Chalcedon abandoned: Roman Catholic theologians

In the previous chapter we have discussed two modern Christologies which proceed from Chalcedon. Both Pannenberg and Moltmann want to retain the confession that Jesus was *vere homo* and *vere Deus*, while at the same time they try to overcome some of the problems involved in the Council's speaking of the two natures in the one person of the Son of God.

There is, however, also an entirely different approach in many present-day Christologies. To put it quite briefly: they reject the Chalcedonian formula of Jesus being true man and true God at the same time, and they quite openly speak of Jesus as man, and no more than man. In his article on 'Present-day Questions in Christology' H. Berkhof mentions three objections to the solution of Chalcedon and in particular to its subsequent en-hypostatical accentuation:[1] (i) the doctrine of the Trinity here moves in the direction of tri-theism; (ii) the historical Jesus, conceived an-hypostatically, that is, without a human person as the ground of his existence, begins to look alarmingly like God dressed up as man, or like a composite being: half God and half man; (iii) the speculative doctrine of *anhypostasis* and *enhypostasis* cannot be a part of the church's proclamation, as is also proved by the fact that this speculative accentuation is entirely missing in the proclamation of the New Testament itself. For all these reasons we have to look for an alternative solution.

It is striking that this search for an alternative Christology is going on in both Roman Catholic and Protestant theology. In fact, there seems to be a growing consensus at this very point. There are, of course, individual differences, but these theologians are all agreed on two things: first, that we have to take our starting-point in the man Jesus; secondly, that we have to take his true humanity absolutely

[1] H. Berkhof, *Rondom het Woord*, November 1973, p. 8.

and ultimately seriously. In this and the following chapter we shall deal respectively with three Roman Catholic and three Protestant theologians.

Piet Schoonenberg

The Dutch theologian Piet J. A. M. Schoonenberg, S. J., for many years professor of systematic theology in the Roman Catholic University at Nijmegen, was one of the leaders of the movement that tried to renew the traditional, mainly scholastic and neo-thomistic theology, by taking into account the results of recent studies in the field of exegetical and biblical theology. In 1969 he published a volume on Christology in Dutch under the title *He is a God of men*.[2] An interesting detail is that this material was originally prepared as a contribution to the multi-volume Roman Catholic standard work on systematic theology, called *Mysterium Salutis*, but the editorial committee rejected it as insufficiently orthodox and replaced it with a contribution by Dietrich Wiederkehr, whose views were much more in line with those of Barth and Pannenberg. Afterwards Schoonenberg's contribution was published as a separate volume, augmented by an extended version of his inaugural lecture, entitled: 'God or man: A False Dilemma'.

His point of departure is a twofold conviction:

1. Jesus is a *unity in himself*. He is one person. This is such a self-evident fact that it is universally accepted. In the books of the New Testament it is so much presupposed that no-one reflects on it.[3] The Council of Chalcedon too takes it as its self-evident starting-point.[4]

2. Jesus is a *real man*.[5] This is just as much a presupposition of the New Testament as the fact that he is one person. His manhood 'comprises all of our existence except sin, thus also positive realities as well as the spiritual soul of man'.[6] At the same time, however, Jesus is different, quite different from us because of his unique relationship with God.

The next question naturally is: What kind of relationship is this? In the Chalcedonian 'pattern' or 'model' he is called a divine person. True, the Chalcedonian formula itself does not use this expression,

---

[2] In 1972 it was published in an English translation, with the title *The Christ*. The change of title is explained in the introduction, p. 8.
[3] *Ibid.*, p. 66.   [4] *Ibid.*, p. 68.
[5] *Ibid.*, p. 71.   [6] *Ibid.*, p. 72.

but it is certainly in line with Chalcedon and therefore it is not at all surprising that we find the expression in theology after Chalcedon, which Schoonenberg calls 'neo-Chalcedonism'.[7] This conclusion was reached via the idea of the pre-existent divine person. 'Jesus Christ is a divine person, for he is personally the same as the eternal Son of the Father, the Second Person of the Most Holy Trinity.' The Christological problem that thus arose was solved via the doctrine of *anhypostasis* and *enhypostasis*. The human nature did not have a *hypostasis* of its own, a human person as the ground of its being (= *anhypostasis*), but from the very beginning of its existence it had its ground in the *hypostasis* of the Logos, the second Person of the Trinity (= *enhypostasis*).

Schoonenberg utterly rejects this solution, for in that case Jesus would not have been a true man. The human subject would have been replaced by the divine subject. But what then is the relationship between this man Jesus and God? Schoonenberg believes that behind many Christological problems lies the idea that God and man are 'rivals'. But this idea (which, for instance, was always very prominent in that part of the doctrine of providence which was called 'concurrence'[8]) is altogether wrong. In Christology we should not operate with the formula 'God *and* man', but we should speak of 'God *in* man'.

But is this enough? Does the New Testament not speak of Jesus Christ in terms of pre-existence, *i.e.* of the Word that was with God before the incarnation and that became flesh? Schoonenberg believes that we should not take the texts about pre-existence literally, but should re-interpret them. We should never forget that everything that is said about Jesus' divinity in his pre-existence is said in connection with the man Jesus Christ, and that nothing is said outside this connection.[9] In other words, we should not take our starting-point in a divine person who subsequently becomes man, but we should start from the man Jesus concerning whom pre-existence is predicated.

This, of course, has a bearing on the doctrine of the Trinity. Here too we should not start with a doctrine of the Trinity, which is

[7] *Ibid.*, p. 75.
[8] *Cf.* L. Berkhof, *Systematic Theology*, 1953, pp. 171ff. Berkhof defines it as follows: 'the co-operation of the divine power with all subordinate powers, according to the pre-established laws of their operation, causing them to act and to act precisely as they do', p. 171. *Cf.* also the first part of Schoonenberg's book: 'God or Man: A False Dilemma', pp. 13–49.
[9] *The Christ*, p. 80.

applied to Jesus, but we should realize that we know of the Trinity only as it became manifest in Jesus Christ and in the Spirit who was sent to us.

To make his own position clear, Schoonenberg then goes on to make use of the very ideas of *anhypostasis* and *enhypostasis*, namely, *by inverting them*! The Word of God, by itself impersonal (= anhypostatical), takes on individuality in the man Jesus Christ (= enhypostatical). 'It is primarily not the human nature which is enhypostatic in the divine person, but the divine nature in the human person.'[10] Schoonenberg believes that in this way he has avoided the pitfalls of traditional Christology. This new Christology is a Christology without duality.[11] It is a Christology of God's presence. In Jesus Christ the whole man is penetrated by God's presence.[12] In this way Jesus is the 'eschatological man', who already stands in the final completion and who from there remains for us not only our example, but also our inspiration, bringer of salvation, life, freedom, love, sonship.[13]

In an article written nearly ten years later Schoonenberg introduced a slight correction. While he did maintain the idea of the *enhypostasia* of the Word in the man Jesus, at the same time he tried to do more justice to what Chalcedon stood for. In the article he compared the *Spirit Christology* and the *Logos Christology*.[14] In the New Testament we find several attempts at a Spirit Christology,[15] but in the course of the first centuries the Logos Christology took the centre. In the nineteenth century (Edward Irving) and in our own century (G. W. H. Lampe)[16] the Spirit Christology was revived. In this Christology the Spirit not only characterizes the whole salvific function of Jesus but also Jesus himself in his sonship with regard to God and to us.[17]

What Schoonenberg appreciates in this type of Christology is that it does justice to the full humanity, especially the human personhood of Jesus. At the same time he sees as its inherent danger the idea of adoptionism, 'for it acknowledges Christ as divine functionally rather than ontologically, or, in the terms of Lampe, adverbially

---

[10] *Ibid.*, pp. 87, 89.   [11] *Ibid.*, pp. 91f.
[12] *Ibid.*, pp. 93f.   [13] *Ibid.*, p. 98.
[14] P. J. A. M. Schoonenberg, 'Spirit Christology and Logos Christology', *Bijdragen* 38 (1977), pp. 350–375.
[15] *Ibid.*, pp. 351f.
[16] *Cf.* G. W. H. Lampe, 'The Holy Spirit and the Person of Christ', in S. W. Sykes and J. P. Clayton (eds.), *Christ, Faith and History*, 1972, pp. 111–130.
[17] Schoonenberg, *art. cit.*, p. 353.

rather than substantively'.[18] In this connection he also makes an adjustment to his own view as set forth above. It is not enough to say that God's presence in Jesus was final. We must also say that it is *reciprocal*.[19] The Logos is not only en-hypostatic in the person of Jesus, but it is equally true that Jesus is en-hypostatic in the Logos. He bases this second aspect on the relationship of God to his creation. 'God, being immanent, also transcends the creature, so that at the same time the creature is present and immanent in God.' This, of course, also applies to the presence of the Logos in Jesus. 'God's Logos, being fully present in Jesus, is also the ground, the *hypostasis*, of Jesus' human reality.' And so Schoonenberg can now affirm with the classical doctrine that the human reality of Jesus is en-hypostatic in the Logos. At the same time, of course, he continues to reject the idea of the *anhypostasis* of the humanity of Jesus.

This addition was undoubtedly caused by a declaration issued in 1972 by the Vatican Congregation for the Doctrine of Faith. This Declaration qualified as an error 'the assertion that the humanity of Christ existed not as being assumed into the eternal person of the Son of God but existed rather of itself as a person, and therefore, that the mystery of Jesus Christ consists only in the fact that God, in revealing himself, was present in the highest degree in the human person Jesus. Those who think in this way are far removed from the true belief in Christ, even when they maintain that the special presence of God results in his being the supreme and final expression of divine revelation. Nor do they come back to the true belief in the divinity of Christ by adding that Jesus can be called God by reason of the fact that in what they call his human person God is supremely present'.[20]

The main question, of course, is whether by the addition of the *enhypostasia* of the man Jesus in the Logos Schoonenberg has really satisfied the demand made by the Vatican Congregation. I believe the answer is in the negative. It is obvious that the Declaration starts from the Chalcedonian idea that the eternal person of the Son of God assumed human nature. In other words, it proceeds from the classical doctrine of the *anhypostasis* and the *enhypostasis*. By taking his starting-point in the human personhood of Jesus, Schoonenberg cannot possibly escape from what the Congregation describes as an error.

The addition he makes (*i.e.* that the *enhypostasia* is reciprocal)

[18] *Ibid.*, p. 361.   [19] *Ibid.*, pp. 364f.   [20] *Ibid.*, p. 363.

does not fundamentally change his basic starting-point. The *enhypostasia* of the man Jesus in the Word is in itself not unique. It is what Jesus shares with all human beings and with the whole creation. The whole emphasis remains on the humanity of Christ. Whatever we may have to say about him (and we have to say a great deal about him, according to Schoonenberg), principally and essentially he is and remains *man*. The basic thrust of Chalcedon is rejected. The uniqueness of Christ is found in the unique indwelling of the Word of God in his humanity. In other words, Schoonenberg cannot go beyond a presence-Christology or a revelational Christology.

Likewise, it is hard to see how he can maintain the essential or ontological Trinity. At any rate, such a Trinity does not exist before the 'incarnation'. On the basis of the Old Testament Schoonenberg does maintain that both the Word and the Spirit were present as 'extensions of person', as 'outpourings of God towards mankind',[21] but not as persons. This they become in uniting themselves with Jesus' human person in this most intimate way.[22] And so, through and in the unique relationship with Jesus, God *becomes* a trinity of persons. Schoonenberg believes that in this way he can maintain the ontological Trinity. It may not be an eternal Trinity, but it certainly is ontological, for God not only *manifests* himself as tri-une, but by *becoming* tri-une he really *is* tri-une in his very essence.

It is evident that this view of the ontological Trinity is quite different from what the church throughout the ages has understood by it. Schoonenberg believes that he can appeal to John's sentence: 'The Word *became* flesh'. In my opinion this appeal is not valid. In the case of the incarnation God acts in history. Admittedly, this also means a change in God's relationship to his creation. In a sense one can even speak of a change in God himself. But the essential or ontological Trinity the church has always understood as what God *is* in his innermost being from all eternity and unto all eternity.

To be sure, this became *manifest* in full clarity only in the incarnation of the Son and the outpouring of the Spirit. But becoming manifest is fundamentally different from 'becoming' in the sense of Schoonenberg's conception. This 'becoming' means that God really changes, not only in his self-revelation and self-communication, but also in his own being. He becomes what he was not before. One can even say that God needs the history of salvation just as much as we do, albeit in a different way.

---

[21] *Ibid.*, pp. 367f. [22] *Ibid.*, p. 368.

We have given so much space to Schoonenberg's view, because he is one of the most outspoken and most consistent Roman Catholic advocates of the alternative Christology. But he is by no means the only one. Several other leading Roman Catholic theologians of our day come very close to his position. It may not be so obvious in their case, because they usually try to maintain the formulations of the ancient councils as well; but they can do this only by a vigorous process of re-interpretation. In most cases they do not really differ from Schoonenberg. I am thinking here in particular of the Christological concepts of Edward Schillebeeckx and Hans Küng.

Edward Schillebeeckx

In recent years Edward Schillebeeckx, who was also professor of systematic theology in the Roman Catholic University at Nijmegen until 1982, has been much in the limelight, owing to the fact that he was called to Rome to submit to an investigation of his theological views. The suspicion centred on his Christological views, which he had expressed in several major works. As a matter of fact, within the space of three years he published two large and important studies on Christology: *Jesus, An Experiment in Christology*[23] and *Christ, The Christian Experience in the Modern World*.[24] In addition he published a shorter work, *Interim Report on the books 'Jesus' and 'Christ'*,[25] in which he tried to clarify some obscurities and remove some misunderstandings. How much Schillebeeckx speaks to his contemporaries and in particular to his fellow-Christians appears from the fact that within six months 12,000 copies of the first book were sold in the Netherlands. The German translation too went through a second printing in a very short time.

In the introduction to the first volume Schillebeeckx clearly states why he wrote the book and why he wrote it the way he did. In his contacts with people he discovered that they often had difficulty in accepting the 'Christ of the Church'.[26] He therefore decided 'to look critically into the intelligibility for man of Christological belief in Jesus, especially in its origin'.[27]

In the first volume he accordingly sets out on the quest for the historical Jesus. It appears to be a long, winding road. In the New

---

[23] Dutch edition in 1974. E.T. 1979 (767 pages!).
[24] Dutch edition in 1977. E.T. 1979 (925 pages!).
[25] Dutch edition in 1978. E.T. 1980 (151 pages).
[26] *Jesus*, p. 34.   [27] *Ibid.*, p. 33.

Testament itself the historical Jesus is overlaid with many layers of interpretation; but by means of the historical-critical methods (here Schillebeeckx relies heavily on recent German traditio-critical research) it is possible to arrive at the picture of Jesus as he met with and was seen by his own contemporaries. This historical Jesus is the final norm and criterion by which all later interpretations have to be tested and checked.

What is the result? We first of all discover that the heart of Jesus' message was the preaching of the kingdom of God.[28] But this message can never be separated from Jesus' own manner of life. Where he himself appears, the sick are healed and evil is banned. Thus people experience Jesus' own caring and abiding presence as salvation coming from God.[29] From the sources it is also clear that Jesus can do this only by his unique relationship with God. In this connection Schillebeeckx gives much attention to Jesus' original *Abba*-experience, which he calls 'the source and secret of his being, message and manner of life'.[30] But was this *Abba*-experience not the grand illusion of Jesus' life? Did his life not end on a cross? Schillebeeckx deals at length with Jesus' rejection and death. But the New Testament testimony does not stop there. After Jesus' death something unexpected and altogether new happened. His disciples had an experience of forgiveness, which they expressed in categories of resurrection.

In the first Dutch edition Schillebeeckx was rather vague about the actual resurrection event. The empty tomb was seen as an *a posteriori* interpretation. The appearances were seen as interpretations of conversion and mission experiences.[31] In the third Dutch edition, however, and in all translated versions a new section was added,[32] which did much to clarify his position. Now he clearly speaks of the resurrection as 'what happened to him, personally, after his death'.

But who, then, is Jesus himself? The earliest interpretation which we can discover, and which must go back to Jesus himself, is that he is the latter-day messenger of God, the eschatological prophet, who is greater than Moses and who offers God's salvation to us.[33] Out of this most basic interpretation afterwards other titles, *i.e.*, interpretations, developed, such as Christ, *Kyrios*, Son of God.[34]

---

[28] *Ibid.*, pp. 140ff.   [29] *Ibid.*, pp. 179ff.   [30] *Ibid.*, pp. 256–269.
[31] *Cf. Ibid.*, p. 385: 'The matrix account of the appearances is no longer recoverable out of the sifting of tradition and redaction'.
[32] *Ibid.*, pp. 644–650. *Cf.* also *Interim Report*, pp. 74ff.
[33] *Ibid.*, pp. 172f., 480ff.   [34] *Ibid.*, p. 480.

Actually they are all confirmations of the basic and original interpretation. The title 'Son of God', for instance, says: 'The final prophet is Son of God because, initiated into God's wisdom, he speaks of and for God to men.'[35]

But what then about the later teaching of Nicea and Chalcedon that Jesus is *vere Deus* and *vere homo* in the one divine Person? In the last part of his book *Jesus*, Schillebeeckx wrestles with these very questions. I must say that it is one of the most difficult parts of the book. Having read the volume so far, one would expect Schillebeeckx to say that Jesus is the unique new man who has a unique relationship with God as his Father, and leave it at that. But in actual fact he goes much further and tries to arrive at a Trinitarian doctrine of God.[36]

This attempt, however, is full of tensions. On the one hand, he vigorously maintains Jesus' humanity. Thus he states that, when the church called Jesus 'the Son', it thereby specified Jesus' creaturely relation to God.[37] On the other hand, he speaks of Jesus' humanity as a humanity in which 'being of the Father' is realized. To put it in another way: it is a real humanity; therefore there is no place for the idea of *anhypostasis*.[38] But at the same time we must speak of *enhypostasis*, for the centre of Jesus' being-as-man was vested not in himself but in God the Father.[39] And so Schillebeeckx comes to a fully-fledged doctrine of the Trinity. Jesus reveals to us 'three persons' in God: Father, Jesus Christ, Pneuma,[40] and this is not only an economic but a really essential Trinity.

This conclusion seems to indicate that Schillebeeckx is after all in agreement with classical Christology and the classical doctrine of the Trinity. It is questionable, however, whether this is so. As to the latter, in an article[41] written in response to a critique of his book by H. Berkhof, Schillebeeckx emphatically states that nowhere in his book does he say that God can be called 'three persons' before the appearance of Jesus. We cannot speak of the Trinity in separation from the Christological interpretation of Jesus. For this very same reason we cannot interpret Jesus himself from the starting-point of the Trinity.[42] At the same time, however, Schillebeeckx maintains that there is in God a 'reality' which precedes and corresponds to

[35] *Ibid.*, p. 498.   [36] *Ibid.*, pp. 652ff.   [37] *Ibid.*, p. 655.
[38] *Ibid.*, p. 656.   [39] *Ibid.*, p. 658.   [40] *Ibid.*, p. 660.
[41] E. Schillebeeckx, 'Fides Quaerens Intellectum Historicum', *Nederlands Theologisch Tijdschrift* 29 (1975), p. 345.
[42] *Jesus*, p. 658.

what became manifest in the appearance of Jesus. But we cannot 'name' this reality before the incarnation.[43] It is God's own secret. At this point Schillebeeckx clearly does not go as far as Schoonenberg, but he comes close to the latter's position.

Whether Schillebeeckx ultimately arrives at the classical Christology is also doubtful. We have already seen that he continually speaks of the humanity of Christ. 'What in non-religious language is called – and rightly so – a *human person*, in the language of faith is called Son of God, by virtue of the constitutive relation of this *human being* to the Father.'[44] We also remember that the doctrine of *anhypostasis* is rejected, although the idea of *enhypostasis* is retained. To what extent, then, can one still speak of agreement with Chalcedon? It may be true that earlier Schillebeeckx has declared that to him, as a Christian, Chalcedon is 'the norm and criterion of Christian belief',[45] but is this really so?

At the end of his third book, *Interim Report on the books 'Jesus' and 'Christ'*,[46] he himself raises the question: 'In your view, is Jesus still God? Yes or No?'[47] It is striking that in his answer he does not really go beyond a functional, revelational Christology. He makes two complementary statements about Jesus: (i) he is the decisive and definitive revelation of God; (ii) in being this he also shows us what we humans can be and should be.[48] Or, to put it in other words, 'in the man Jesus the revelation of the divine and the disclosure of true, good and really happy men and women . . . completely co-incide in one and the same person'.[49] Schillebeeckx claims in the closing lines of the book that this is the same as what Nicea and Chalcedon tried to say in the concepts of their time. Here we have our doubts. We believe that what he says actually is more in line with Schoonenberg than with the councils. The latter spoke not merely in terms of 'revelation' and 'disclosure' but in terms of 'being'. Jesus himself, in his own being, is truly God and truly man. In him we meet with God himself, because he truly (*vere*) shares in God's divinity. In him we also see the true man, because he also truly (*vere*) shares in our humanity.

It must be granted, of course, that this difference between Schille-

---

[43] *Art. cit.*, p. 345.   [44] *Jesus*, p. 655, my italics.   [45] *Ibid.*, p. 484.
[46] We do not deal separately with the second volume, *Christ, The Christian Experience in the Modern World*, not because we regard it as unimportant (as a matter of fact, it contains many beautiful expositions of New Testament soteriology, apart from the Synoptic Gospels), but because it does not contribute new aspects as far as our present discussion is concerned.
[47] *Interim Report*, p. 140.   [48] *Ibid.*, p. 142.   [49] *Ibid.*, p. 143.

beeckx and the ancient councils does not yet determine the correct-
ness or incorrectness of Schillebeeckx' views. Theoretically at least,
Schillebeeckx might be closer to the way in which the New Testament speaks about Jesus, for it is obvious that the councils spoke in
the theological (and philosophical) language of the fourth and fifth
centuries. Schillebeeckx' own studies are primarily of an exegetical
nature. By a historical-critical analysis of the New Testament itself
he tries to discover who Jesus really was in his relation to both God
and man.

But at this very point we also encounter the real problem of
Schillebeeckx' method. We can put it in the form of the following
question: To what extent are we today bound to the interpretations
of Jesus' person as given by the various writers of the New Testament? In Schillebeeckx' own thinking there is a tension here. In an
earlier work he stated that the first New Testament models in which
Jesus came to us are normative.[50] But in recent years he has moved
beyond this position by stating that as believers we are bound only
to 'what comes to expression in Jesus'.[51] But how do we know what
comes to expression in Jesus?

Schillebeeckx himself tries to answer this question by searching
for the historical Jesus, who is the final norm and criterion by which
all later interpretations have to be tested and checked. But this
historical Jesus whom Schillebeeckx claims to have found is the result
of his own research; and that, in turn, is determined by his own
starting-point, namely, that we have to see Jesus' historical manifestation within the quite specific ongoing tradition in which he and his
contemporaries were set: the horizon of experience which we now
call the Old Testament and, even more specifically, its late Jewish
or Judaistic context.[52] But this means that from start to finish Schillebeeckx' historical Jesus is interpreted in categories of Jewish-func-
tional theology. And since this historical Jesus is the final norm and
criterion by which all later interpretations must be tested and
checked, it is not surprising to see that the whole New Testament
itself is also interpreted in functional categories.[53] Concepts such as

---

[50] E. Schillebeeckx, *Geloofsverstaan: interpretatie en kritiek*, 1972, p. 103.

[51] *Cf.* T. J. van Bavel, 'Hermeneutische knelpunten in een theologisch dispuut'
(latente veronderstellingen in de stukken van de 'zaak Schillebeeckx'), *Tijdschrift voor
Theologie* 20 (1980), p. 349. Schillebeeckx himself is managing editor of this journal.
The issue referred to is entirely devoted to Schillebeeckx' theology and the 'trial' in
Rome.

[52] *Jesus*, p. 104.

[53] *Cf. Ibid.*, p. 556. *Cf.* also *Christ*, pp. 168ff. (on Phil. 2) and pp. 353ff. (on Jn. 1).

Son of God and pre-existence cannot be essential categories any more. So the road to Nicea and Chalcedon is automatically blocked.[54]

Hans Küng

The same is regrettably true of the Christology of another famous Roman Catholic theologian, Hans Küng. He is famous, not only because of his numerous major works, but also because of his conflict with Rome, resulting in his dismissal as teacher of Roman Catholic students in the University of Tübingen. Since his influence is considerable, also in Protestant circles, we shall discuss his view at somewhat greater length.

For a proper understanding of Küng's theology it is necessary to realize that he first of all wishes to be an apologist of the Christian faith, in a world which is involved in an increasing process of secularization. In a letter to bishop George Moser of Rottenburg-Stuttgart he wrote: 'Both in the past and the present, I proceed on the assumption that our common faith in Jesus Christ must be expressed in such a way that it can be understood not only by theologians, practising Catholics and evangelical Christians, but also by the numerous questioning people outside the Church.'[55] This means for him that we must abandon the old, medieval world picture and accept the picture that has arisen out of modern science.[56] What is called for is a new paradigm, a consistent reorientation, with all its consequences for the doctrine of God, the doctrine of man, the Christology, ethics, eschatology, etc. The consequences for the doctrine of Christ he has discussed at length in his last two major works, *On Being a Christian*[57] and *Does God Exist?*[58]

From both works it is evident that he opts for a Christology 'from below'. Having stated that Jesus Christ himself is the distinctive feature, and also the programme, of Christianity, he asks the questions: 'Who is this Jesus? What did he want?'[59] The answer is to be found primarily in the Synoptic Gospels, which must be read in the

[54] It must be borne in mind that Schillebeeckx' Christology is as yet unfinished. The third, more dogmatic volume is still to appear.

[55] *Concilium*, 1980, no. 8 (Dutch edition), p. 88.

[56] Hans Küng, *Does God Exist?*, 1980, p. 115.

[57] German edition in 1974. E.T. 1976. We quote from the Collins Fount Paperback, 1978.

[58] German edition in 1978. E.T. 1980.

[59] *On Being a Christian*, p. 177.

light of modern historical criticism. Thus it is accepted that Jesus himself did not assume any titles implying messianic dignity: not Messiah, nor Son of David, nor Son, nor Son of God. All these titles were given to him afterwards by the Christian community, when it saw him in the light of the paschal faith.[60] And yet this man, who is not supported by any special descent, family, education, retinue or party,[61] raises a stupendous claim: he demands from every one who meets him 'a final decision for God's cause and man's',[62] and he asserts a 'completely underived, supremely personal authority'.[63] This finally leads to his death on the cross. But his death is not the end. Shortly afterwards his disciples discover that 'the Crucified lives'.[64] This discovery becomes the starting-point for a new development: Jesus' own person becomes the concrete standard for God's kingdom.[65]

Thus an explicit Christology emerges from the implicitly Christological speech, action and suffering of Jesus himself. In fact, we see several diverse Christologies emerge in the New Testament.[66] We also see how several diverse honorific titles are given to him: Son of man, Messiah-Christ, Lord, Son of God, Logos. They are all messianic titles, some of which developed an important dynamism of their own.[67] Take, for instance, the title 'Son of God'. Originally this title 'had *nothing to do with Jesus' origin but with his legal and authoritative status. It is a question of function, not of nature'. It did not refer to a corporeal sonship, but to divine election and authorization, as in the case of Israel's king who also was the representative of God. Yet Jesus was more than representative in the legal sense only. He was such 'as personal messenger, trustee, indeed as confidant and friend of God'. Having been exalted to God's right hand, he appeared to be 'in the definitive and comprehensive sense – "once for all" – *God's representative* to men'.[68]

This *exaltation Christology* (*i.e.* the Christology 'from below')[69] was increasingly superseded by an *incarnation Christology* (*i.e.* a Christology 'from above'). Strictly speaking we may find it only in the Gospel of John, but it cannot be denied that the idea also occurs in Pauline writings (Phil. 2:6–11; Gal. 4:4; 2 Cor. 8:9; Rom. 8:3; Tit. 2:11; 2:4).[70] The ascendance Christology is replaced by a de-

---

[60] *Ibid.*, p. 289. *Cf. Does God Exist?*, p. 682.
[61] *Ibid.*, p. 290.   [62] *Ibid.*, p. 291.   [63] *Ibid.*, p. 293.
[64] *Ibid.*, p. 357.   [65] *Ibid.*, p. 384.   [66] *Ibid.*, p. 385.
[67] *Ibid.*, p. 389.   [68] *Ibid.*, p. 390, Küng's italics.   [69] *Ibid.*, p. 439.
[70] *Ibid.*, pp. 437f.

scendance Christology, leading to the idea of an ontological generation.[71] For Hellenistic hearers 'Son of God' becomes a pre-existent, superhuman being of divine origin and with divine power. Yet Jesus is hardly ever called 'God' (never by Paul himself in his own, authentic writings!) and there is no mention in the New Testament of an incarnation of God himself. Only in John's Gospel do we hear Thomas' exclamation: 'My Lord and my God!'[72] It was Greek theology that drew conclusions from the new Hellenistic conception of divine sonship, leading to an increasing concentration on the incarnation.

What is Küng's own view? He clearly opts for a 'functional Christology', as distinct from an 'essence Christology'.[73] Jesus' relationship to God should be expressed in categories of 'revelation'. Jesus is *'God's word and will in human form'*.[74] 'The true man Jesus of Nazareth is for faith the real *revelation* of the one *true God.'*[75] In Jesus God shows us who he is, shows us his face. In this sense Jesus is the Image, the Word, the Son of God. Within this same context, pre-existence, as attributed to Jesus, means that he has always been in God's thought[76] and that the relationship between God and Jesus existed from the beginning and has its foundation in God himself.[77]

There can be no doubt that this is a functional Christology indeed. But does this agree with what the ancient church confessed at the councils of Nicea, Ephesus and Chalcedon? Küng believes that the answer is positive. To be sure, the councils expressed themselves in metaphysical terms (*homoousios*, 'of the same substance'), but they could not do otherwise, because there was simply no other conceptual system available.[78] Yet what they stood for, the *vere Deus* and the *vere homo*, should be maintained in our day too. 'That God and man are truly involved in the story of Jesus Christ is something to be steadfastly upheld by faith even today.'[79]

But what does the *vere Deus* mean in Küng's conception? He gives the following interpretation:

[71] *Ibid.*, p. 439.   [72] *Ibid.*, p. 440. *Cf. Does God Exist?*, pp. 684f.
[73] *Ibid.*, p. 448.   [74] *Ibid.*, p. 443, Küng's italics.
[75] *Ibid.*, p. 444.   [76] *Ibid.*, p. 445.
[77] *Ibid.*, p. 446. *Cf.* the quotation from Frans Mussner in *Does God Exist?*, p. 684: 'The christological doctrine of preexistence in regard to the man and prophet Jesus of Nazareth proclaims nothing other than *Yahweh's* always, "from eternity", *being-there-for*, which was definitely revealed in the man Jesus of Nazareth – "revelation" incidentally being understood in the strictest sense of the word.'
[78] *Ibid.*, p. 448.   [79] *Ibid.*, p. 449.

The whole point of what happened in and with Jesus depends on the fact that, for believers, *God himself* as man's friend was present, at work, speaking, acting and definitely revealing himself *in this Jesus* who came among men as God's advocate and deputy, representative and delegate, and was confirmed by God as the Crucified raised to life. All statements about divine sonship, pre-existence, creation mediatorship and incarnation – often clothed in the mythological or semi-mythological forms of the time – are meant in the last resort to do no more and no less than substantiate the *uniqueness, underivability and unsurpassability* of the *call, offer and claim* made known in and with Jesus, ultimately not of human but of divine origin and therefore absolutely reliable, requiring men's unconditional involvement.[80]

As to the *vere homo*, he says that Jesus was *wholly and entirely man*, a *model of what it is to be human*, representing the *ultimate standard of human existence*.[81] He believes that in this way nothing is deducted from the truth taught by the councils. It is only transferred to the mental climate of our own time.[82]

Evaluation

It is evident from this brief summary that Küng's Christology is a well-structured and consistent piece of theology. His decisive starting-point is the 'historical Jesus' as 'discovered' by modern historical-critical exegesis. This leads to a Christology 'from below', a line which is consistently followed to the very end. He does not deny, of course, that the New Testament also speaks of a Christology 'from above' (an incarnation Christology); this second line, however, is not seen as complementary to the first, but is subordinated to and actually regarded as an extension of the original exaltation Christology. At no stage is the idea of incarnation seen as the ultimate statement about who Jesus really is. In *Does God Exist?* he reiterates that Jesus is hardly ever directly called God and never at all by Paul.

---

[80] *Ibid.*, p. 449, Küng's italics.
[81] *Ibid.*, pp. 449f., Küng's italics.
[82] *Ibid.*, p. 450. It is not surprising to read that for Küng the virgin birth is no more than an aetiological legend of saga. 'The theologoumenon of the Son of God is thus vividly portrayed as history: the theologoumenon has been turned into a mythologoumenon', p. 456; *cf.* pp. 450ff.

We find such expressions 'only in a few, all likewise late, Hellenistically influenced exceptional cases'.[83] Therefore, today we should call Jesus 'Son of God' rather than simply 'God' and, as to the term 'incarnation', we should not relate it only to Jesus' birth or conception but rather to his *life and death as a whole*.

What this means is explained in the following statement:

> God's becoming man in Jesus means that in all Jesus' talk, in his whole proclamation, behavior and fate, God's word and will have assumed a human form. In all his talking and action, suffering and death, in his whole person, Jesus proclaimed, manifested, revealed God's word and will. He, in whom word and deed, teaching and life, being and action completely coincide, *is* in person, *is* in human form, God's Word, will, Son.[84]

As we can clearly see, Küng again does not go beyond a *functional* statement. True, he asserts in the next sentence that functional and ontological statements must not be torn apart. One can even say that in the statement quoted an attempt is made to express Jesus' person in ontological categories. But it is also evident that the ontological terminology does not really go beyond the functional, and it does not surprise us that in the following sentence we again read that Jesus is 'the *revelation* of God's power and wisdom'.[85] Perhaps one could say that in Küng's Christology ontological language is 'functionalized'.

In a lengthy review of *On Being a Christian*, Richard Bauckham has called this 'a kind of naïve biblicism'.[86] Bauckham does not deny that New Testament Christological language is primarily (though not entirely) functional. But this functional Christology requires further reflection; and, once reflective questions are asked about it, it appears to demand an essential Christology to back it up. But, of course, at that stage a return to a naïve functional Christology is no longer possible. One cannot pretend that these questions have never been asked. Küng can escape only by declaring that the maturer fruits of Christological reflection in the New Testament (pre-exist-

---

[83] *Does God Exist?*, p. 685. It is hardly possible to depreciate these texts in a more derogatory fashion. The question is not even raised whether these texts might be a legitimate development of earlier statements.
[84] *Ibid.*, p. 685.   [85] *Ibid.*, p. 685, my italics.
[86] *Themelios* 4 (1979), no. 2, p. 74.

ence, incarnation, mediation in creation) belong to mythological ways of thought which must be discarded.[87] But is this not a highly unscientific way of treating material that does not fit into one's own preconceived scheme?

It is not surprising either to see that Küng has difficulty in squaring his own view with that of the ancient councils, especially with the *vere Deus* and the *vere homo* of Nicea. In fact, he appears to be greatly angered by the German Bishops' Conference which had accused him of denying the Christological statements of the Nicene Creed. He rejects this accusation utterly. He does admit to preferring functional terminology to the Hellenistic terminology used by the Fathers. But in his opinion it is not the terminology used that is decisive, but the reality attested in the New Testament: Jesus Christ himself. Now what did Nicea want to say about this reality? Over against Arius, who wanted to introduce a concealed polytheism into Christianity, the council 'made clear that the one true God was wholly present and active in Him. With the Fathers of Nicea, we are convinced that our whole salvation depends on the fact that in Jesus we are concerned with the one God, who is truly, really and alone God: in Jesus as His Son made evident'.[88]

It cannot be denied that here wonderful things are being said about Jesus. But it cannot be denied either that this is less than what Nicea said. Nicea undoubtedly also believed that Jesus was *the* revelation of God. But it went on to say that he is the revelation of God, *because* he is the Son of God in an ontological sense: 'of the same substance with the Father'.

Küng refuses to go beyond the general statement: 'God in Jesus Christ',[89] and then adds: '*In this sense* we agree also with the Council of Nicea in 325, when it speaks of Jesus Christ as "God from God, Light from Light, true God from true God, begotten, not made, of one Being with the Father".'[90] But this, of course, is playing with words and obscuring the real issue. 'God in Jesus Christ', in a revelational sense, was *not* the issue of Nicea. As a matter of fact, this was gladly acknowledged by Arius, who was condemned by the same council! Nicea wanted to say more. Jesus is 'true God from true God', that is, the Second Person in the Trinity, 'made man, for us and for our salvation'.

---

[87] *Does God Exist?*, p. 792, note 11.
[88] *Ibid.*, p. 687.   [89] *Ibid.*, p. 685.
[90] *Ibid.*, p. 685, my italics.

Such language Küng cannot really use. Admittedly, his own terminology quite often comes very near to incarnational language, but
at the decisive moment he draws back and refuses to go beyond
revelational language. This appears quite clearly from the personal
confession he makes in *Does God Exist?* It is worth quoting in full.

> For me, Jesus of Nazareth is the *Son of God*. For the whole
> significance of what happened in and with him lies in the fact
> that in Jesus – who appeared to us men as God's advocate,
> deputy, representative and delegate, and who, as crucified and
> raised to life, was authenticated by God – the God who loves
> men is *himself present and active*: through him, God himself
> has spoken, acted, definitively revealed himself. . . .
> I want to maintain firmly the uniqueness, underivability and
> unsurpassability of his person and the appeal, offer and claim
> there made articulate. Since God himself definitely speaks and
> acts through him, he is for me the Christ of God, his
> revelation and his likeness, his Word and his Son. He and no
> other, he as the only one, 'only-begotten', *unigenitus*. . . .
> I can maintain firmly that Jesus precisely as Son of God,
> without any qualifications and with all the consequences, was
> *wholly and entirely man*, could suffer just like other men, felt
> loneliness and insecurity, was not free from temptations,
> doubts and errors. But, as distinct from myself and all other
> human beings (including saints and founders of religion), he is
> not a mere man, but *the* true man precisely as God's Word
> and Son.[91]

I deeply respect this confession which comes from the heart. Here
speaks a man of genuine faith in a language that appeals to the soul.
One therefore hesitates to analyse and criticize it. But even a genuine
confession which comes from the heart is not beyond analysis and
criticism. When analysing it, one cannot fail to notice the following:
(i) this confession does not go beyond the revelational level; (ii)
while he does interpret the *vere homo*, without any qualification, as
'*wholly and entirely man*', the *vere Deus* is *not* interpreted in the
same unqualified way as 'wholly and entirely God'. Yet this was the
real concern of Nicea. The *vere Deus* and the *vere homo* were both
predicated of the one Jesus Christ. Küng does not wish to go

[91] *Ibid.*, p. 688.

beyond the statement which we quoted before: 'The *true man* Jesus of Nazareth is for faith the real *revelation* of the one *true God*.'[92] Here the *vere Deus* is no longer the predicate of Jesus himself. He is 'only' the *revelation* of the *vere Deus*.

It is no wonder that the doctrine of the Trinity is also interpreted functionally rather than essentially. In the final analysis Küng cannot go beyond the statement that 'the unity of Father, Son and Spirit is to be understood as *revelation event* and *revelational unity*'.[93] We do not deny that this is an important and also a true statement, but we also notice that it speaks of an economic rather than of an essential unity. The same is found in *Does God Exist?* Jesus is the representative of God and at the same time, as man, the representative of men.[94] The Spirit is the representative on earth of the risen Christ.[95] Again, it is an economic, revelational unity only. But, of course, this does not surprise us any more, after the analysis of his Christology. For, as he remarks on the last page, 'the trinitarian question has developed out of the christological question'.[96]

---

[92] *On Being a Christian*, p. 444.   [93] *Ibid.*, p. 477.
[94] *Does God Exist?*, p. 700.   [95] *Ibid.*, p. 701.
[96] *Ibid.*, p. 702.

Chapter Six

Chalcedon abandoned:
Protestant theologians

When in this chapter we turn to the views of some Protestant theologians who virtually follow the same road, things become much clearer. Not encumbered or inhibited by the claims of an infallible tradition, Protestant scholars are more apt and willing to reconsider the traditional Christology and venture upon new pathways.

In all the Christological concepts under review here, the results of the historical-critical exegesis of the New Testament, in particular the new quest for the 'historical Jesus', appear to have given the impetus to a thoroughgoing reconsideration and reconstruction of the traditional Christology. Another striking feature is that none of them denies that in the New Testament itself we do find Christologies 'from above'. In fact, they all believe that this approach 'from above' is indispensable as a complementary aspect to the Christology 'from below'. Yet, in the final analysis, the Christology 'from below' appears to be decisive.

As examples I again mention three names, which I take in chronological order of their major publications in this area.

Ellen Flesseman

The first example is the book *Believing Today*,[1] written by the Dutch theologian Dr Ellen Flesseman and published in 1972. It is a popular dogmatics, based on solid research, in which the author tries to restate the Christian doctrines in the light of modern biblical exegesis and *en rapport* with contemporary thinking. Characteristic of her Christology is not only the fact that she begins with the 'historical Jesus' (chapters IX and X), but also that she sees him strictly against the background of the Old Testament. Jesus is the true partner in the covenant that God established with Israel for the sake of the world.[2]

---

[1] Dutch title: *Geloven vandaag.*   [2] *Believing Today*, p. 99.

But who is this Jesus, the true covenant partner? Is he, as the ancient creeds state, very God and very man at the same time? Flesseman cannot accept this. Although she appreciates the intentions of the creeds and even admits that they protected the ancient church against deviations that would obscure our salvation, she nevertheless has serious objections. The creeds virtually make Jesus into a being that is both God and man. But this is impossible. Just as Schoonenberg, she wants to drop the formula 'God *and* man' from Christology and replace it by speaking of 'God *in* man': 'God's presence *in* this man'.[3] Accordingly, the New Testament title 'Son of God' must be interpreted as an indication of the exceptional relationship that existed between God and this man Jesus. 'Because Jesus lives in an absolute relationship with God, God also wants to have full fellowship with him. Because Jesus is so completely "true man", God also wants to be one with him. Therefore we can speak about Jesus only by using two words. In him we are confronted with a man who realized the God-given destiny of humanity – and in him we are at the same time confronted with God.'[4]

It is obvious that Flesseman cannot accept the doctrine of incarnation. She does not deny that this idea is present in the writings of Paul and John, who by means of it want to express that in Jesus Christ God himself has come to us.[5] But this concept is no longer suitable for our day. Moreover, it reminds us too much of all kinds of mythological stories. Yet, there is an important truth in the New Testament's speaking about Christ in incarnational terms, namely, that 'God has the initiative in the history of Jesus Christ'.[6] For this reason he can also be the source of our salvation.[7] At this point Flesseman, like all the other advocates of the new alternative Christology, differs sharply from the older liberal theologians in the tradition of Adolf von Harnack. For her Jesus is the Redeemer. The secret of his life and death is that he reconciled us with God. But this does not alter the fact that in her opinion he was man, and no more.

Naturally, she can no longer hold to the doctrine of the Trinity either. In fact, she is very consistent and also very outspoken on this point. 'I cannot believe in a trinitarian God, as if there would be a three-ness in Him: God the Father, God the Son and God the Holy Spirit. The Son Jesus Christ is not God, but a man who was so one

---

[3] *Ibid.*, p. 95.   [4] *Ibid.*, p. 98.   [5] *Ibid.*, p. 101.
[6] *Ibid.*, p. 102.   [7] *Ibid.*, pp. 104f.

with God that in him I meet God; and the Spirit is not an entity beside God the Father, but he is God Himself, communicating to me Himself, the power of his presence, the power of his holy love. That is why I cannot speak of a trinity within God. And yet I do have to speak about Him in a trinitarian fashion, for I need three words to speak about the encounter with Him.'[8] Three words: 'I encounter (that is the Spirit) God (that is the Other, the Creator) in the man Jesus Christ (that is the Son).'[9]

John A. T. Robinson

The second example is the Christology of John A. T. Robinson, who in 1973 published his book *The Human Face of God*. Robinson, who is widely known as the iconoclastic author of *Honest to God*,[10] was by profession a New Testament scholar and therefore naturally interested in the matter of Christology. Yet his real concern is not just academic but, rather, existential. He wants to write about it as one who is vitally interested in the subject and wants to communicate it to his own contemporaries. 'Indeed, my concern . . . is to a large extent with self-questioning – with *how today* one can truthfully and meaningfully say (in the words of the earliest and shortest Christian confession), "Jesus is Lord". I shall be writing as one who *wants* to make that confession. "For", as Paul said of himself, to those who have known it "the love of Christ leaves us no choice". I cannot step out of my skin. For "to me life is Christ".'[11] And so he embarks on a new quest for the answer to the question what it means to call Jesus 'the Christ'. This question cannot be answered by simply repeating biblical or credal phrases. 'For Jesus Christ to be "the same yesterday, today and for ever" he has to be a contemporary of every generation, and therefore different for the men of every generation. He must be *their* Christ.'[12]

His basic starting-point, which is of a dogmatical/philosophical rather than an exegetical nature, is found in the first sentence of the second chapter: 'If Jesus as the Christ is to be our man, he must be one of us: *totus in nostris*, completely part of our world . . . ; in other words, a man in every sense of the word.'[13] But this is only the starting-point. From it he tries to penetrate into more than just the human dimension of Jesus' being. The order of the chapter

[8] *Ibid.*, p. 125.   [9] *Ibid.*, p. 125.
[10] First published in 1963.   [11] *The Human Face of God*, XI.
[12] *Ibid.*, p. 16.   [13] *Ibid.*, p. 36.

headings indicates the path he follows: Our Man, A Man, The Man, Man of God, God's Man, God for Us, Man for All.

These headings clearly show that Robinson does not opt for a 'low' Christology. In fact, he confesses to plead for 'the highest possible Christology in relation *both* to the humanity *and* the divinity of Christ'.[14] He does not hesitate to say that God dwells in Christ 'as in a son' and 'that this indwelling was by personal union and not just by intermittent grace'.[15] This is 'high' language indeed.

However, in order to understand this language properly, we should constantly remember that Robinson opts for a functional approach. Following the Dutch philosopher, Cornelis van Peursen, he distinguishes two major shifts in the history of human thinking: (i) from myth to ontology; (ii) from ontology to functional thinking.[16] These shifts can also be observed in the developments in Christology. First there was the transition from Jewish categories (finality is seen in terms of the eschatological act of God in history, embodied in the sending of his Messiah as saviour and judge of everything) to Greek categories (the Christ is described in terms of being/substance rather than of will). In recent years we see a new shift from the ontological to the functional, which means that we must start from Jesus as *'this man*, a genuine product of the evolutionary process with all its random mutations'.[17] He calls it the *'sine qua non* of personal existence, namely, the nexus of biological, historical and social relationships with our fellow-men and with the universe as a whole'.[18] If this was not true of Jesus, he would only have been a 'visitor'.

Robinson naturally has no place for a doctrine of two natures united in the one divine Person,[19] nor for the patristic doctrine of the *anhypostatos* and the *enhypostatos*.[20] The 'formula' he himself presupposes is that of:

> one human person of whom we must use two languages, man-language and God-language. Jesus is wholly and completely a man, but a man who 'speaks true' not simply of humanity but of God. He is not a man plus, a man fitted, as it were, with a

---

[14] *Ibid.*, p. 141.   [15] *Ibid.*, p. 205.
[16] *Ibid.*, p. 33.   [17] *Ibid.*, p. 34; *cf.* pp. 148, 200.
[18] *Ibid.*, p. 41. So Jesus must have had 'all the pre-history of man in his genes', p. 42, 'genes and chromosomes shaped and transmitted by millions of years of evolution', p. 43. He must have 'belonged to one particular blood-group' and 'had the characteristics of one psychological type rather than another', p. 69.
[19] *Ibid.*, pp. 109f.   [20] *Ibid.*, pp. 147f.

> second engine – which would mean that he was not a man in any genuine sense. He is a man who in all that he says and does as man is the personal representative of God: he stands in God's place, he *is* God to us and for us.[21]

In this one sentence we have Robinson's whole Christology in a nutshell. Superficially it looks very much like the Chalcedonian doctrine of the two natures, and yet it is entirely different. While the Council of Chalcedon asserted that Jesus *was* both God and man at the same time, Robinson says only that we have to use *two sets of language* about the one man Jesus.[22] In the one case we speak empirical language, which is natural, scientific and descriptive,[23] and we say: he is a man, just as we are. In the other case we use the language of faith, which is supernatural, mythological and interpretative, and we say: this man is God's personal representative – more than that, he *is* God to us and for us. In both cases the word 'is' is used, but it is used in different senses or, if you wish, on different levels. This 'double-talk' characterizes Robinson's whole Christology.

So he interprets Paul's statements, 'God sent his own Son, born of a woman, born under the law' (Gal. 4:4), and 'by sending his own Son in a form like that of our own sinful nature' (Rom. 8:3), as follows: This is 'the picture of a man born like the rest of us, from within the nexus of the flesh, law and sin, who nevertheless embodied the divine initiative and saving presence so completely that he was declared at his baptism and confirmed at his resurrection to be everything God himself was – his Son, his power and his wisdom, his image, his fullness'.[24]

All such expressions, however, should not be taken in an 'essential' sense. Robinson definitely does not want to go beyond a functional Christology. It is true that, time and again, he uses ontological language, yet this very language must be understood functionally. Jesus is 'a human figure raised up from among his brothers to be the instrument of God's decisive work and to stand in a relationship to him to which no other man is called. The issue is whether in seeing him men see the Father, whether, in mercy and judgment, he *functions* as God, whether he *is* God to and for them'.[25] The 'is' and the 'functions' are not identical, but the 'is' must be interpreted in the light of the 'functions'. Within this functional framework very 'high'

[21] *Ibid.*, pp. 113f. [22] *Ibid.*, p. 116. [23] *Ibid.*, p. 117.
[24] *Ibid.*, p. 162. [25] *Ibid.*, p. 184.

language can be used. Jesus is called 'to *be* God's decisive word to men, the embodiment of his nature and the enactment of his will'.[26] He 'represents the definitive revelation of God'.[27] His response is not 'simply that of the prophet to declare the word of God, but to *be* the word of God, to act and speak as *God for us*'.[28] But such language never goes beyond the functional. Consequently, when forced to choose, Robinson opts for a 'degree Christology',[29] that is, Jesus differs from us in degree only, not in essence.[30]

Hendrikus Berkhof

The third and in my opinion most important example of the new alternative Christology among Protestant theologians is to be found in the book *The Christian Faith*,[31] by Hendrikus Berkhof, former professor of systematic theology in the University of Leyden. The chapter on 'Jesus the Son' is perhaps the most penetrating analysis and re-interpretation of the traditional Christology that has appeared in recent years. Unfortunately, we can give only a short summary, which means that we cannot possibly do justice to the refined way in which the author handles the many intricate aspects of the Christological question.

In the first section Berkhof states that actually there are four possible approaches in the Christology:[32] 1. *from behind* – here we see Jesus in the line of redemptive history, *i.e.*, in line with the Old Testament; 2. *from above* – here we see how in him the creative Word of God becomes a historical human life; 3. *from below* – here we see him as a human being within the framework of his own time; 4. *from before* – here we see him from the perspective of what he has worked out through the centuries. All four approaches are complementary.

Berkhof himself prefers to start with the approach 'from below', *i.e.*, he starts off with the so-called historical Jesus. He is well aware of the fact that historical-critical research cannot bring to light the divine secret of Jesus the Christ; but he also believes that, if there is such a secret, we shall sooner or later, in one way or another, hit

---

[26] *Ibid.*, p. 197. [27] *Ibid.*, p. 221.
[28] *Ibid.*, p. 210. [29] *Ibid.*, p. 209.
[30] For a helpful discussion of Robinson's view, see Norman Anderson, *The Mystery of the Incarnation*, 1978, pp. 95–107.
[31] Original Dutch edition in 1973. E.T. 1979.
[32] *The Christian Faith*, p. 267.

upon it and then we shall have to seek for a different, more deeply penetrating approach.[33]

Having made this choice he proceeds to examine the New Testament sources. In a summary he gives the following picture of the historical Jesus:

> Jesus was . . . convinced that in his offer of grace the Kingdom itself was already present in a provisional form. This conviction rested on a most intimate relationship with God whom he, very intimately, addressed as 'Father', and it manifested itself in a speaking with an unheard-of 'authority', a declaring of God's will without an appeal to earlier authorities.[34]

Whether Jesus used messianic titles for himself or not, one thing is clear: there must have been in him an 'implicit Christology', on which the post-Easter community could build interpretatively. It is, however, not easy to get a clear view of this 'implicit Christology'. In fact, the closer we come to the actual situation, the more we realize that the secret of Jesus does not yield itself up, but becomes even more mysterious. We discover that, just like Peter, we have to make a personal choice and a personal confession 'You are the Christ'. At that very moment we find a new coherence and perspective: 'The Old Testament, John the Baptist, his passion and death, his resurrection, his new mode of existence as the living Lord – everything is joined together in the one continuous covenantal way of God with his people, on which Jesus Christ turns out to be God's great and definitive step toward his future and to us.'[35]

This is also the moment that Berkhof switches from the approach 'from below' to that 'from behind': Jesus as the fulfiller of the way of Israel. In this context he discusses the many names accorded to Jesus in the New Testament. The most adequate of these is the title 'Son of God', which is a redemptive-historical concept. In the Old Testament both Israel itself and its king are called God's son. This has nothing to do with physical origin, but is indicative of a covenantal relationship. Jesus' sonship also stands in this covenantal tradition. 'He is pre-eminently the obedient and therefore beloved covenant partner.'[36]

However, this insertion of Jesus as the Son of God into the

[33] *Ibid.*, p. 268. [34] *Ibid.*, p. 276.
[35] *Ibid.*, p. 280. [36] *Ibid.*, p. 283.

(historical) course of the covenant should not make us lose sight of the fact that within this context his sonship is 'entirely unique'. He is not only one of the long chain of covenant partners, but he also stands opposite the others. In the preceding history of the covenant, sonship has come to a dead end, which means that a new beginning was necessary. At this point Berkhof adopts the third approach: that 'from above'.

A new beginning is necessary, and the prophets know that this cannot be expected from below. God himself must provide the true man, the faithful covenant partner. That new beginning from above is called 'Jesus'. He finally fulfils the sonship. He is the Son *par excellence.* And he is that not as the fruit and climax of human religious and moral purity, but in virtue of a unique and new creative act of God. Therefore, there is between Father and Son not only a covenantal relationship, but also a relationship of origin, a new covenantal relationship based on a unique relationship of origin. Jesus is therefore the son, the 'only-begotten' Son. . . . He the Son in a pre-eminent sense, in whose God-created relationship with God the covenant is renewed and forever established: *Immanu-El,* God with us.[37]

As this Son, he is the true representative who in his radical covenantal obedience breaks open for all the others the way to the full, definitive, eschatological salvation.

But *who is he in himself?* Is he God or man or both at the same time? Berkhof rejects the formulae of both Nicea and Chalcedon. According to him, Jesus is 'man, the perfected covenant man, *the* new man, the eschatological man'.[38] But does not the New Testament put him, as the Son, on the side of God? Indeed, this is true. But we should also remember that the New Testament nowhere pictures him as a dual being. He is the new covenant man who lives in a thus far unknown oneness with God.

There are . . . not two subjects in Jesus, but his human 'I' is, out of free will, fully and exhaustively permeated by the 'I' of God; and in virtue of this permeation he becomes the perfect instrument of the Father. This completed covenant relation-

[37] *Ibid.,* p. 283.   [38] *Ibid.,* p. 287.

73

ship signifies a new union of God and man, far beyond our experience and imagination.

This union is, however, not something static; it passes through a history. Jesus starts his covenantal way as the carpenter's son from Nazareth, and finally, after much inner turmoil and struggle, he ends by fully participating in the life of the Father and in his work in the world. The exclusive sphere of God, the 'glory' (Heb. *kābôd*; Gr. *doxa*), passes in Jesus to *one* man. God does not push the human person of Jesus aside, but he permeates it entirely with his Spirit, that is, with himself. So in the obedient and therefore resurrected and glorified Jesus our humanity far transcends what we can imagine and even consider covenantally possible. In that transcendence humanity in its covenantal relationship to God is, however, not obliterated but brought to its highest fulfilment.[39]

It is quite understandable that Berkhof cannot accept the decision of Chalcedon and the subsequent doctrine of the *anhypostasis* and the *enhypostasis*. According to him, both do injustice to the full humanity of Jesus and obstruct the way to the Jesus of the Gospels. We should abandon this static framework of two natures as two structures on top of each other, but rather think historically, *i.e.*, 'on the way of a progressive obedience and glorification Jesus exhibits more and more new and to us unknown dimensions of the divinely intended humanity'.[40]

It is obvious that Berkhof has no place either for the idea of pre-existence in an ontological sense. The passages that seem to speak of it are all re-interpreted.[41] Concerning John 1, Colossians 1 and Hebrews 1, he categorically declares that they do not really speak of it. Philippians 2 offers more difficulties, but it is also removed from the list, because it is seen as on a par with Jewish ideas of the pre-existence of the Torah and wisdom. In other words, it is a mythical form of what today we would call 'ideal pre-existence': God's first and dominant thought in his plan of creation and salvation was Jesus the Son.[42]

In a similar vein, the virgin birth is seen as a later embellishment of the tradition, which was used to indicate 'that Jesus, the Son by

---

[39] *Ibid.*, p. 287.
[40] *Ibid.*, p. 288.
[41] *Ibid.*, p. 289.
[42] Cf. *Ibid.*, p. 292.

pre-eminence, did not arise out of the empirical human world, but is a new creation which man cannot bring forth but only receive'.[43]

Nor is it any longer possible, of course, to speak of a real incarnation. All passages that use incarnational language (the Word becoming flesh, God sending his Son or Jesus being called 'God') must be seen as 'capturing in an accentuated formula Jesus' uniqueness and instrumentality relative to us'.[44] In other words, it is all a matter of 'covenantal functionality': Jesus is seen as 'the representative of God in the world and in history'.

Finally, this view also has far-reaching consequences for the doctrine of the Trinity. This doctrine too has to be re-interpreted and seen in terms of covenantal, relational thinking. The three names, Father, Son and Holy Spirit, 'do not constitute *one* being in eternity, but *one* history in time'.[45] The Trinity is an event, not *in* God, but arising *from* God and leading *to* him. It is an event in which God extends and carries on his own life so as to share it with man.[46] The Father is the divine Partner, the Son is the human representative, the Spirit (who is God-in-relation) is the bond between Father and Son and therefore also between the Son (with a capital S) and all the other sons whom he draws to the Father.

Some brief comments

Since it is impossible to evaluate Berkhof's whole Christology, it must suffice to offer only a few brief comments.

1. Berkhof's view shows a remarkable degree of *affinity* with that of the other theologians discussed in this and the previous chapter (with the exception perhaps of Robinson). He himself is aware of this and mentions the names of Schoonenberg and Flesseman.[47]

2. His own concept proves that historical investigation, which is characteristic of the approach 'from below', is indeed unable to uncover the divine secret of Jesus Christ. Even the addition of the approach 'from behind' is not enough to uncover this secret. For even when we acknowledge Jesus as the fulfilment of God's covenant with Israel and therefore as *the* covenantal representative, he still remains human and no more.

3. Berkhof is aware of this and therefore also adds an approach 'from above'. He describes Jesus as 'the beginning from above'[48] and

---

[43] *Ibid.*, p. 293. [44] *Ibid.*, p. 290. [45] *Ibid.*, p. 331.
[46] *Ibid.*, p. 332. [47] *Ibid.*, p. 291. [48] *Ibid.*, p. 283.

speaks of 'a unique and new creative act of God', 'a new covenantal relationship based on a unique relationship of origin'. Within this context he has no difficulty in calling Jesus *the* son, the Son *par excellence*, the 'only-begotten' Son, and in speaking of him as the *Immanu-El*,[49] to whom the exclusive sphere of God, the *kābôd* (glory) of God, has been given.[50] He can even say: 'God was in Jesus'.[51] But however 'high' the language he uses may be, he always stops short at calling Jesus God's Son in an ontological sense. There is in Jesus a divine secret, but it is not the secret of his own divinity!

4. Does this mean that Berkhof's concept, too, is no more than a functional Christology? He himself appears to be rather uncomfortable with the dilemma ontological/functional. This appears, for instance, from the fact that he refuses to answer the question once posed by Bultmann: 'Does he help me because he is the Son of God or is he the Son of God because he helps me?' Berkhof regards this as a false dilemma. In our cultural situation we cannot go back to the one-sided ontological mode of thought of years ago, but at the same time we must realize that a purely functionalistic way of thinking leads us nowhere.[52] In an article, in which he replied to some of the critics of *Christian Faith*, he wrote that 'substance' and 'function' belong together as 'side and reverse-side'[53] and therefore cannot be separated. Further on in the same article he put it thus: 'The functionality of the new covenantal man is grounded in an ontological secret.'[54] Indeed, this is the core of Berkhof's Christology. It is not *merely* functional, for Jesus is seen as the Son in virtue of a unique and new creative act of God. The relationship between Jesus and the Father is not only of a covenantal nature, but is based on a relationship of origin.[55] Yet it cannot be denied either that throughout the entire section on Christology the real emphasis is on the function, and that the titles given to Jesus in the New Testament (including that of 'Son of God') are primarily interpreted in a functional sense. When a few times Jesus is called 'God', we must understand this in terms of 'covenantal functionality'.[56] Yes, even the expressions which have an ontological bearing (such as 'a unique relationship of origin') serve as an indication of the special character of the work Jesus does as 'the perfected covenant man, *the* man, the eschatological man'.[57]

[49] *Ibid.*, p. 283.   [50] *Ibid.*, p. 287.
[51] *Ibid.*, p. 308.   [52] *Ibid.*, p. 285.
[53] H. Berkhof, 'Weerwoord op de Ru en Geense', in *Kerk en Theologie* 26 (1975), p. 318.
[54] *Art. cit.*, p. 320.   [55] *The Christian Faith*, p. 283.
[56] *Ibid.*, p. 290.   [57] *Ibid.*, p. 287.

Ultimately one wonders whether there really is an essential difference between Jesus and, for instance, Moses or David or Isaiah, and whether Berkhof really succeeds in going beyond a 'degree Christology'. For Jesus may transcend the boundaries of what we understand by 'human', but ultimately he does no more than exhibit new, and to us unknown, dimensions of the divinely intended humanity.[58] And even when Jesus' own life ends in the full participation in the life of the Father and his work in the world, he himself never transcends this divinely intended *humanity*.[59]

5. The real crux of the matter seems to be that Berkhof *uses the New Testament data selectively*. In the article from which we quoted before, he quite frankly admits that he replaces the Johannine *Logos*-model by a kind of *Pneuma*-model. According to him we cannot avoid a choice/selection, because the New Testament itself is so pluriform at this point. Such a selection does not matter, as long as the methodical consistency is safeguarded and we can bring out other additional elements of the unspeakable reality of salvation. The fundamental question, of course, is whether the model used by John (and also by Paul and the writers of Hebrews, who with John are *the* representatives of the approach 'from above') is just 'a' model that can be discarded and replaced at will. Or does it represent the most comprehensive and inclusive model, which is able to incorporate all the valuable elements of other models, while the latter models are too limited to include the fundamental concern of the incarnational model? Or, to put it in another way, once Jesus' coming has been revealed in terms of incarnation, can one still go back to earlier levels of understanding and deal with 'incarnation' as just one of the many models which are at our disposal?

[58] *Ibid.*, p. 287.   [59] *Ibid.*, p. 288, my italics.

Chapter Seven

The debate about
The Myth of God Incarnate

In the late 1970s a debate on the incarnation took place in the United
Kingdom. It started with the publication of the volume *The Myth
of God Incarnate* in 1977 by seven British theologians. The book
created quite a stir, mainly, one suspects, because of its provocative
title, for in actual fact it did not contain much that was new. Most
of its ideas had been propounded in earlier publications, either by
the authors themselves[1] or by others.[2] In the same year an answer
was given by a number of evangelical theologians in the small volume
The Truth of God Incarnate,[3] while the Anglican vicar, George
Carey, wrote the booklet *God Incarnate*. In the following years the
debate continued. In 1978 a colloquy was held between the original
seven essayists and a group of their leading critics. The results were
published in the symposium *Incarnation and Myth*, subtitled 'The
Debate Continued'.[4]

The first question we have to ask is: Why was this debate started?
In the common introduction to *The Myth of God Incarnate* the
seven authors state that they wrote their essays, not only for the
sake of truth but in particular also 'to make Christian discipleship
possible for our children's children'.[5] All of them are of the opinion
that the doctrine of the incarnation, when taken as a description of
factual truth, is no longer 'intelligible', a word that often occurs in
the volume. In the opening essay Maurice Wiles asks: 'Are we sure
that the concept of an incarnate being, one who is both fully God

---

[1] *E.g.*, M. Wiles, *The Remaking of Christian Doctrine*, 1974, and John Hick, *God
and the Universe of Faith*, 1973.

[2] This is frankly admitted by Michael Goulder in *Incarnation and Myth*, VII.

[3] Edited by Michael Green.

[4] Published in 1979 and edited by Michael Goulder. In the same year Don Cupitt
(one of the seven essayists) also published his *The Debate about Christ*. Understand-
ably the original volume also evoked a spate of articles and reviews on both sides of
the Atlantic Ocean.

[5] *The Myth of God Incarnate*, X.

and fully man, is after all an intelligible concept?'[6]

But how then do the authors see Jesus? In the Preface they describe as their common starting-point the conviction that 'Jesus was (as he is presented in Acts 2, 21)[7] "a man appointed by God" for a special role within the divine purpose, and that the later conception of him as God incarnate, the Second Person of the Holy Trinity living a human life, is a mythological or poetic way of expressing his significance for us'.[8] This sentence, actually consisting of two separate statements, also indicates the main content of the book, which consists of two parts: I. 'Testing the Sources', and II. 'Testing the Development'.

In the first part Frances Young and Michael Goulder look at the sources, that is, the New Testament data and early patristic references. From this combination it is already apparent, as John Stott has pointed out,[9] that the contributors do not recognize the New Testament as authoritative and therefore have no objective standard or criterion by which to test their own views. Frances Young argues that the Christological titles derive from the surrounding cultural background and were used by the early Christians to express their faith-response to Jesus of Nazareth.[10] Moreover, there are quite a number of different Christologies in the New Testament.[11] Some New Testament authors, Paul for instance, use incarnational language; yet even Paul's Christology is not really incarnational.[12] In her summing up Dr Young maintains that the traditional doctrine of the incarnation is read into, not out of, the Pauline Epistles. At the same time she also admits

> that it is more than remarkable that Jesus should have stimulated such a far-reaching response from so many different quarters. . . . All manner of men found their salvation in him and were driven to search for categories to explain him, never finding any single one adequate, always seeking higher ways of honouring, worshipping and understanding him. . . . Even though he is not directly confessed as *God*, yet the confessions used do show that he 'stands for' God, and is the focus through which God is revealed to those who respond.[13]

---

[6] *Ibid.*, p. 5.   [7] This should be Acts 2:22.   [8] *Ibid.*, IX.
[9] John R. W. Stott, 'Is the Incarnation a Myth?', *Christianity Today*, November 4, 1977.   [10] *The Myth of God Incarnate*, p. 18.
[11] *Ibid.*, p. 19.   [12] *Ibid.*, p. 21.   [13] *Ibid.*, p. 22.

Her own solution is to think of Jesus in two 'models'. The first one is the 'scientific model', which finds explanations in terms of natural causes. The second one is the 'mythological or symbolical model', which, however inadequate, represents the religious and spiritual dimension of our experience.[14]

(a) The story of a *man* who lived as the 'archetypal believer', who lived and died trusting in God, and accepted the bitter consequences of the stupidity of such a career and his inevitable failure.
(b) The story of *God* being involved in the reality of human existence with its compromises, its temptations, its suffering, its pain, its injustice, its cruelty, its *death*; not running away from it, not pretending that all this does not exist, but transforming its darkness into light, demonstrating that he takes responsibility for all that seems wrong with the world that he created.[15]

Within the context of these two stories Young herself can also use 'high' Christological language and say: 'I see God in Jesus', and 'God was in Christ reconciling the world to himself'. But this does not alter the fact that for her Jesus is 'a real man in the human context'.

In the second part of the volume Leslie Houlden and Don Cupitt discuss the doctrinal development leading to Nicea and Chalcedon. Both reject this development as a deviation from what the New Testament tells us about the historical Jesus. Houlden distinguishes between 'experiential' language, which tries to describe the surging spring of inspiration, and 'credal' language, which turns this spring into a controlled flow of thought.[16] In Part II we also find another contribution from Maurice Wiles on 'Myth in Theology' and one contribution from the editor, John Hick, who argues that the doctrine of incarnation, when taken literally, is pernicious, because it 'implies that God can be adequately known and responded to *only* through Jesus; and the whole religion of mankind, beyond the stream of Judaic-Christian faith is thus by implication excluded as lying outside the sphere of salvation'.[17]

This short summary cannot, of course, do justice to the volume under discussion. The contributions of Frances Young and Maurice

[14] *Ibid.*, p. 34.   [15] *Ibid.*, p. 37.
[16] *Ibid.*, p. 128.   [17] *Ibid.*, p. 179.

Wiles are well worth reading and pondering. Yet we must say that the volume as a whole is rather disappointing, as will appear from the following comments.

1. There is much repetition and little cohesion in the volume. At times one suspects that the doctrine of the incarnation simply had to be repudiated and that both the New Testament data and the subsequent doctrinal developments are read from the perspective of this preconceived repudiation.

2. Although the term 'myth' is used in the title of the book, there is no unanimity among the authors as to its exact meaning. In fact, each one seems to have his own interpretation. In his second contribution, which is devoted to the subject 'Myth in Theology', Wiles admits (i) that various contributors to the volume have used it in different ways; (ii) that the term itself has a 'loose and elusive character'.[18] He himself seems to understand myths as expressions of 'certain fundamental aspects of the human condition'.[19] He further maintains that 'there must be some ontological truth to the central characteristic of the structure of the myth'.[20] He has no difficulty in recognizing this in the myths of creation and fall. But what about the incarnation? Is it not much more difficult to use the term 'myth' here, because it is tied up with a historical person, the man Jesus of Nazareth? The only way out for Wiles is to 'generalize' the whole idea of 'incarnation' by wrenching it from its concrete historical mooring and to describe it as something 'which makes possible a profound inner union of the divine and the human'.[21] This is the experience of all individual believers. It is also the experience of the church as a whole (which has frequently been spoken of as 'the extension of the incarnation'). And Jesus, with his openness to God, experienced it in a very special manner. Now this interpretation of the term 'myth' is quite interesting; within its own context it makes sense. But it is also obvious that nothing is left of a real incarnation of the Word of God in Jesus. In his case, too, it is only a matter of an 'inner union of the divine and the human at the heart of the human personality'. In Jesus this union may be more profound than in all other human beings before and after him. But essentially it is not any different from that which we ourselves also experience.

3. The authors generally show a deep and unwarranted scepsis as to the historical reliability of the New Testament writings. Quite often the data are re-interpreted in such a way that little or nothing

[18] *Ibid.*, p. 148. [19] *Ibid.*, p. 159.
[20] *Ibid.*, p. 161. [21] *Ibid.*, p. 161.

is left of the original meaning. It is striking that the resurrection of Christ plays hardly any role at all. Only two authors deal with it explicitly. John Hick explains it as 'some kind of experience of seeing Jesus after his death', but then adds that we 'cannot ascertain today in what this resurrection-event consisted';[22] Michael Goulder explains it entirely psychologically:[23] on Easter morning 'the amazing truth dawned on him [Peter], to solve all his problems: Jesus was not dead after all – he had risen again. . . . So great is the power of hysteria in a small community' that in the evening the other disciples went through a similar experience. One cannot help feeling amazed that this old theory has been revived (or, should we say, resurrected?) and one cannot but agree with Ellen Flesseman when she comments that this interpretation by means of mass hysteria is at least as miraculous as the biblical interpretation![24]

4. The volume is also almost entirely silent about the soteriological significance of Jesus. A few times the atoning effect of Jesus' life and death are mentioned, but we are not informed by the authors what they mean by the term 'atonement'. This is not surprising when we see that sin and guilt are hardly mentioned at all. The only exception is Frances Young who recognizes that 'salvation and atonement are the core of the Christian message',[25] and then goes on to make a moving personal confession:

> Faith demands a doctrine of atonement, and atonement means a conviction that God has somehow dealt with evil, with sin, with rebellion; that on the cross, God in Christ entered into the suffering, the evil and the sin of his world – entered the darkness and transformed it into light, into blazing glory; that God himself took responsibility for the existence of evil in his creation, that he bore the pain of it and the guilt of it, accepting its consequences into himself; that he in his love reconciled his holiness to a sinful and corrupt humanity, justifying the ungodly, accepting man just as he is.[26]

I find this a very moving account and am sure that every evangelical will whole-heartedly agree with this confession. Then I see that

---

[22] *Ibid.*, p. 170.   [23] *Ibid.*, p. 59.

[24] E. Flesseman-van Leer, 'Christologische discussie in Engeland', *Kerk en Theologie* 33 (1979), p. 127.

[25] *The Myth of God Incarnate*, p. 34.   [26] *Ibid.*, p. 35.

Young immediately adds that 'to say this kind of thing is to use poetic, anthropomorphic or "mythological" language; it is not to present a theological conclusion based on logical argument'. But what then does her confession mean, especially when on the next page she says that mythological language not only is 'inevitably inadequate' but also 'certainly not literally true'?[27] Is the cross to her (and to the other authors) indeed nothing but 'a Calvary-centred religious myth'?[28]

5. At some stage Frances Young admits that there are 'incarnational elements' in the New Testament.[29] She also admits that 'there does not seem to be a single, exact analogy to the total Christian claim about Jesus in material which is definitely pre-Christian; full scale Redeemer-myths are unquestionably found AD but not BC'.[30] Yet she remains convinced that incarnational belief belongs naturally enough to a world that was accustomed to supernatural ways of speaking. As examples she mentions the phrase 'son of God', the idea of the ascent of an exceptional man to the heavenly realm, and belief in heavenly beings or intermediaries who might descend to succour men. These ways of speaking, she argues, would almost naturally lead to the idea of a genuine incarnation of such a heavenly being. But then she has to admit that 'here the analogies become inadequate'. In other words, it is to all appearances a genuinely Christian conception, which had its origin in the Christian community. And yet, the whole argument again ends with the statement: 'Whether or not we can unearth the precise origins of incarnational belief, it is surely clear that it belongs naturally enough to a world in which supernatural ways of speaking seemed the highest and best expression of the significance and finality of the one they identified as God's awaited Messiah and envoy.'[31] This kind of attitude is typical of the whole volume. The decisive point apparently is not that incarnational belief is absent from the New Testament, but that the authors cannot accept it on extra-biblical, *i.e.*, philosophical grounds.

6. All authors admit that Jesus is someone very special and that he is indispensable to them. At times they speak of him in glowing terms. According to Maurice Wiles, Jesus has taught people 'the truth of God's self-giving love', and he should be seen 'not only as one who embodies a full response of man to God but also one who expresses and embodies the way of God towards men . . . ; the

[27] *Ibid.*, p. 36.   [28] *Ibid.*, p. 34.   [29] *Ibid.*, p. 19.
[30] *Ibid.*, p. 118.   [31] *Ibid.*, p. 119.

power of God was set at work in the world in a new way through his life, ministry, death and resurrection'.[32] Frances Young says: 'I see God in Jesus', and 'Jesus will always be the unique focus of my perception of and response to God'.[33] She even says that Jesus 'stands for' God[34] and that a Christian believer can say only: 'He is "as-if-God" for me.'[35] Michael Goulder believes in 'the unity of activity of God and Jesus'[36] and Leslie Houlden speaks of 'the centrality of Jesus for all that concerns man's understanding of God'.[37] Finally, John Hick says he believes in 'the immense significance of our encounter with one in whose presence we have found ourselves to be at the same time in the presence of God'.[38] Yet they all refuse to speak of him in absolute and exclusive terms. This is no longer possible, now that Jesus' '*metaphysical* uniqueness' (Dennis Nineham)[39] has been given up. All that is left is a 'functional' Christology, in which Jesus is seen 'as the main figure through whom God launched men into a relationship with himself so full and rich that under various understandings and formulations of it, it has been, and continues to be, the salvation of a large portion of the human race'.[40] Again, this is undoubtedly 'high' language, but for all its highness it resolutely avoids speaking of Jesus as unique.

7. Consequently, most authors opt for a religious pluralism. Even when Jesus is seen as Saviour, he is never more than one of the many saviours. He may be central and unique for Christians, but, as Frances Young puts it, 'to claim that Jesus as the cosmic Christ has the same ultimate significance for all mankind irrespective of time, place or culture, is surely unrealistic'.[41] For this very reason John Hick rejects the doctrine of the incarnation, for it 'implies that God can be adequately known and responded to *only* through Jesus',[42] and that 'the large majority of the human race so far have not been saved'.[43] He himself believes that God's self-revelation can assume various forms. For this idea he appeals to the ancient *Logos*-doctrine, on the basis of which 'we should gladly acknowledge that Ultimate Reality has affected human consciousness for its liberation or "salvation" in various ways within the Indian, the Semitic, the Chinese, the African . . . forms of life'.[44] Naturally, there is no need any more for evangelism or mission work. We do not have to convert

---

[32] *Ibid.*, p. 8.   [33] *Ibid.*, pp. 37f.   [34] *Ibid.*, p. 22.

[35] *Ibid.*, p. 39.   [36] *Ibid.*, p. 62.   [37] *Ibid.*, p. 132.

[38] *Ibid.*, p. 184.   [39] *Ibid.*, p. 194.   [40] *Ibid.*, pp. 202f.

[41] *Ibid.*, p. 41.   [42] *Ibid.*, p. 179.   [43] *Ibid.*, p. 180.

[44] *Ibid.*, p. 181.

the adherents of other religions. All we have to do is to share our mutual religious insights and ideals.[45]

8. The greatest weakness of the volume under discussion, as John Macquarrie has pointed out in a short but penetrating review,[46] is that the authors are united only in their dissatisfaction with traditional doctrines of incarnation, but have no common reconstruction of belief to offer. 'Inevitably, therefore, the impression produced is negative and reductionist.'[47] In other words, the book does not really offer an alternative, but virtually revives the old liberal position of the nineteenth century, here and there augmented with a few adaptations which make it more palatable for the post-Barthian era.[48]

The Christology of Process theology

Although this Christology cannot be simply identified with the views propounded in *The Myth of God Incarnate*, there is sufficient basic similarity to warrant a brief discussion of it as an appendix to this chapter. Process theology, taking its cue from the philosophies of Alfred N. Whitehead and Charles Hartshorne, proceeds on the assumption of a pan-en-theistic conception of God. 'God is operative in the whole creation, at every level of existence; he moves through it, works upon it, accomplishes his good will in it.'[49] Yet God is not identical with the creation; he also transcends it. He is undoubtedly *in* the world, but it is equally true to say that the world is *in* him. 'He is the unexhausted and unexhaustible Reality who works through all things, yet ever remains himself.'

What then is the relationship between Jesus Christ and God? If God works in and through all things, how must we conceive of his working in and through Jesus? More than any of the other process theologians, Norman Pittenger has given thought to this question. In the volume just quoted he describes Jesus Christ as the 'focus' of the pervasive and universal activity of God. He is 'the focal manifestation in man' of God in action.[50] Rejecting the idea of a literal incarnation as 'incredible and impossible', he opts for the idea that in Jesus 'the energizing and indwelling of God by mutual inter-

---

[45] *Ibid.*, p. 182.
[46] *The Truth of God Incarnate*, pp. 140–144.   [47] *Ibid.*, p. 144.
[48] It is striking that the name of Karl Barth is nowhere mentioned in the entire volume. For the authors the Barthian era apparently is no more than an interlude between the old and the new liberalism.
[49] Norman Pittenger, *God in Process*, 1967, p. 17.   [50] *Ibid.*, p. 20.

penetration of the divine and the human reaches a climactic stage'.[51]

A few years later Pittenger worked these ideas out in more detail in his book *Christology Reconsidered* (1970). In the first chapter he summarizes his view in three points: (i) in some fashion we meet God in the event of Jesus Christ; (ii) God is thus met in a genuine, historically conditioned, and entirely human being; (iii) God and this man are in relationship with each other in the mode of the most complete interpenetration.[52] This event of Jesus Christ and the complete interpenetration that took place in him can be called 'incarnation', but then in a metaphorical sense only. Incarnation is not limited to the man Jesus either. As a matter of fact, the 'event' of Jesus Christ also includes the long Jewish preparation and the subsequent Christian community.[53] The man Jesus is the centre of this event, because he is 'a unity in whom God and man are brought together in singular intensity'.[54] One can also say that he is 'the One in whom God actualized in a living human personality the potential God-man relationship which is the divinely-intended truth about every man'.[55] It is quite understandable that for Pittenger the difference between God's activity in Jesus and that in the affairs of other men is a difference of degree rather than of kind.[56] It is also understandable that for him the love of God is 'decisively but not inclusively' available in Jesus Christ.[57] Consequently, next to the at-one-ing of God and man through the work of Jesus Christ, there are other at-one-ings.[58]

It is striking how close the views of Pittenger and Maurice Wiles appear to be. Wiles also describes the incarnation as a general event, namely, as 'that which makes possible a profound inner union of the divine and the human in the experience of grace in the life of the believer now and more broadly in the life of the church as a whole'.[59] Secondly, he is also willing to admit that Jesus' life embodied this unity and that therefore it is quite appropriate to link the incarnation myth in this special way with the person of Jesus.[60] Undoubtedly, there are also differences between Pittenger and Wiles; but these are not in kind but only in degree, and it is not surprising to see that the two authors quote each other approvingly.[61]

[51] *Ibid.*, p. 26. *Cf.* also Charles Birch, *Nature and God*, 1965, pp. 72f., 102, 105, 111, 114.
[52] *Christology Reconsidered*, p. 7.   [53] *Ibid.*, p. 86; *cf.* pp. 70ff., 76ff.
[54] *Ibid.*, p. 99.   [55] *Ibid.*, p. 114; *cf.* also the final chapter.
[56] *Ibid.*, pp. 111f.   [57] *Ibid.*, p. 107.
[58] *Ibid.*, p. 96.   [59] *The Myth of God Incarnate*, p. 161.
[60] *Ibid.*, pp. 162f.   [61] *Ibid.*, pp. 154f. *Christology Reconsidered*, pp. 4ff.

Chapter Eight

The New Testament
and the new Christologies

From the foregoing chapters it is quite clear that in recent years there have been many shifts in Christological thinking. There appears to be a general dissatisfaction with the classical Christology, as was also the case in the liberal theology of the nineteenth century. Yet it would be a simplification to say that the new Christological conceptions are a simple return to, or repetition of, the older liberal views, which were all basically humanistic and had no place left for real salvation. Admittedly, some of the newer conceptions come rather close to the older liberal views. This is especially true of the authors of *The Myth of God Incarnate*. But even among them we find Frances Young's moving personal confession of God who in Christ entered into the suffering, the evil and the sin of his world and who transformed the darkness into light, into blazing glory.[1]

Similar confessions are made by other writers. Norman Pittenger ends his book *Christology Reconsidered* with the following personal confession: 'An old man, as years go, may be permitted to say that for him Jesus Christ as the divine Love en-manned, and thus made available to us, is utterly central, as the master-light of all our seeing and the fountain from which living waters may be drunk'.[2] Hendrikus Berkhof makes the following confession in a lecture given to the European Division of the World Alliance of Reformed Churches in 1973:

> You are the true Man, as God has intended you to be from the beginning: the true obedient Son, the man of love, the one who was willing, taking the full consequences, not to maintain his life, but to lose it for others, and who by that exceptional life of love and obedience started in our world the counter-movement of resurrection. And as the true Man you are the

[1] See p. 82, above. [2] *Christology Reconsidered*, p. 153.

Man of the Future. You are not only a strange exception, which would mean merely an accusation directed at us. God has given you as the Pioneer and Forerunner, as the Guarantee that by your sacrifice, your resurrection and your spirit, the future is opened to our rebellious and enslaved race.[3]

I am sure that all Evangelicals share the sentiment expressed in these words. They believe with Berkhof that Jesus Christ is the Pioneer and Forerunner, the Guarantee who by his sacrifice, resurrection and spirit has opened the future to us, rebellious and enslaved people.

It may be salutary at this very point to remind ourselves that the confession of Christ as Saviour and the Christology, which a person holds, *are not simply identical.* Of course, the two cannot be separated from each other either. Each confession of Christ implies a certain Christology, and each Christology leads to a certain confession. Yet the two are not identical. The confession is a matter of personal faith. With it the confessor's being a Christian stands or falls, and it is decisive for his eternal future (*cf.* Mt. 10:32f.; Mk. 8:38f.). The Christology is the doctrine of Christ. It is the systematic reflection upon Jesus Christ and his work, upon who he is and what he has done for us. A man's Christology may be defective, while nevertheless he puts all his trust, for the present and the future, in Jesus Christ, whom he acknowledges as his Lord and Saviour. I for one believe that people like Berkhof fall within this category, however much I may disagree with their Christology.

It is also true that orthodox Evangelicals, while holding to classical Christology, can learn much from these new Christologies. As we have seen, it is characteristic of most of them that they strongly emphasize the humanity of Christ. Our first reaction is perhaps to say that they over-emphasize it. But is it not equally true that Evangelicals often tend to under-emphasize Christ's humanity?

In a paper given to the Fellowship of European Evangelical Theologians in 1980, R. T. France pointed out that 'at least in popular [evangelical] piety there is a strong tendency to a form of unacknowledged docetism, a Jesus about whom the "real" truth is that he is God and whose humanity is a convenient temporary vehicle, but not to be taken very seriously when it comes to discussing the possible

---

[3] Hendrikus Berkhof, 'Who do you say that I am?', *The Reformed World* 32 (1973), p. 303.

limitations on his knowledge or his power, or the degree of his conditioning by the cultural milieu of first-century Palestine'. But when we study the New Testament we cannot but conclude that the biblical picture of Jesus is that of 'a real man, with real emotions and human reactions, who had to learn obedience to the will of God, and did not find it easy, whose knowledge was limited, and who lived and spoke as a first-century Palestinian Jew. All this belongs to the essential raw materials of a Christology which claims to be based on the evidence of the New Testament'.

No doubt all the proponents of alternative Christologies will whole-heartedly agree with this. Their own starting-point is the 'historical Jesus', as portrayed in the Gospels, and they want to develop a complete Christology from this starting-point. But is this really possible? Can they, in this way, ever do justice to the full portrait of Jesus, as we find this in the New Testament?

The New Testament

It is evident to everyone who knows the New Testament that it nowhere offers a full-scale Christology à la Nicea and Chalcedon. Nowhere does it speak of a union of two natures, a divine and a human nature, in one divine Person. Even the term 'incarnation' does not occur in the New Testament. Frances Young may be willing to grant that 'incarnational language' does occur in the New Testament, but other theologians (and they are by no means more 'liberal' than Frances Young) are much more cautious on this point. R. E. Brown, the well-known American Roman Catholic theologian, is of the opinion that the incarnation is truly characteristic of Johannine Christianity, but not of about 90% of the remainder of the New Testament.[4] J. D. G. Dunn goes even further and affirms that John 1:14 is 'the first, and indeed only such statement in the New Testament'.[5]

But, then, what kind of Christology does the New Testament provide? Those who take their starting-point in the 'historical Jesus' usually conclude that Jesus was a man, and no more. Of course, they all admit that he was a special man, who had a unique relationship with God. But this unique relationship does not alter the fact

[4] Cf. I. Howard Marshall, 'Incarnational Christology in the New Testament', in Harold H. Rowdon (ed.), Christ the Lord, Studies in Christology presented to Donald Guthrie, 1982, p. 1.
[5] J. D. G. Dunn, Christology in the Making, 1980, p. 241.

that he was no more than a man. Such a conclusion is not the result of a simple reading of the New Testament (such a reading would rather lead us into a different direction), but is based on *presuppositions* which are connected with certain forms of historical-critical research.[6]

The first presupposition is the idea that it was customary in the first century to represent one's religious ideas in the form of myths or mythological concepts. The second is the conviction that by the use of precise, critical methods we can now actually trace the steps from a relatively simple Jesus and his simple message to the complicated theological Christ of the Gospels and the involved doctrine of redemption. In other words, the New Testament would offer us a picture of an *evolutionary* Christology.

In recent years this evolutionary concept has been seriously contested by C. F. D. Moule. He does not deny that there has been growth within New Testament Christology, but maintains that this growth was not a matter of evolution but rather of development. By 'development' he means that the more explicit Christological statements in the New Testament were not 'successive additions of something new, but only the drawing out and articulating of what is there'[7] from the beginning. According to him 'the evidence . . . suggests that Jesus was, *from the beginning*, such a one as appropriately to be described in the ways in which, sooner or later, he did come to be described in the New Testament period – for instance, as "Lord" and even, in some sense as "God". Whether such terms in fact began to be used early or late, my contention is that they are not evolved *away*, so to speak, from the original, but represent the development of true insights into the original'.[8]

It is a matter of fact that throughout the whole New Testament we find indications of a high Christology. Actually, *all* Christological statements in the New Testament are high. Graham Stanton rightly remarks: 'Judged by later standards parts of the New Testament may seem to reflect a very "low" christology, but in a first-century Jewish context those same affirmations about Jesus may have been extremely bold and even quite unprecedented.'[9] All writers, one way or another, put Jesus on the side of God. At times he is even called 'God'. Admittedly, the latter happens only rarely.

[6] *Cf.* B. Ramm, 'Shrinking the Son of God', *Eternity* 31 (April 1980), p. 26.
[7] C. F. D. Moule, *The Origin of Christology*, 1977, p. 3. [8] *Ibid.*, p. 4.
[9] Graham Stanton, 'Incarnational Christology in the New Testament', in *Incarnation and Myth*, p. 152.

Apparently the attribution of divine attributes to Jesus came slowly and reluctantly. But that, of course, is not surprising at all, when we remember that, with one or two exceptions, all New Testament writers were Jews, brought up in a most stringent monotheism. For them to speak of Jesus in terms of divinity was virtually impossible. And yet it happened! Only one explanation is possible here: this kind of Christology must have had its origin 'in Christian experience of Jesus, both in his earthly ministry and in his risen power'.[10]

This also explains why we find this high Christology already in the earliest writings in the New Testament, namely the letters of Paul. Whether we take the first letter to the Thessalonians as the oldest document or the letter to the Galatians, in each case it was written less than twenty years after the death and resurrection of Christ. Actually we must assume that the period was even shorter, since it is unlikely that 'Paul thought up his Christology on the spot at the time of writing his letters'.[11] Such a rapid development of a high Christology can be explained only by the impact Jesus himself must have made on his followers. They must have been deeply impressed, not only by what he said and did, but also by who he was.

For the source of such a development O. Cullmann,[12] J. Jeremias[13] and others point to Jesus' own self-consciousness, especially his filial consciousness.[14] Cullmann believes that 'in his teaching and life Jesus accomplished something new from which the first Christians had to proceed in their attempt to explain his person and work'.[15] R. H. Fuller is of the same opinion, as appears from his affirmation of 'a direct line of continuity between Jesus' self-understanding and the church's christological interpretation of him'.[16] It was this self-understanding of Jesus and the way he expressed it, in both his words and his deeds, that eventually led to his crucifixion (cf. Mt. 26:63f.; Mk. 14:61f.; esp. Lk. 22:70).

Does this mean that already during his earthly ministry his disciples understood him to be the Son of God in an incarnational sense?

[10] R. T. France, 'The Worship of Jesus: A Neglected Factor in Christological Debate?', in *Christ the Lord*, p. 33.
[11] I. Howard Marshall, *The Origins of New Testament Christology*, 1976, p. 40.
[12] O. Cullmann, *The Christology of the New Testament*, 1959, p. 5.
[13] J. Jeremias, *New Testament Theology* 1, 1971, pp. 56–61.
[14] I. Howard Marshall, *op. cit.*, pp. 114f.   [15] O. Cullmann, *loc. cit.*
[16] R. H. Fuller, *The Foundations of New Testament Christology*, 1965, p. 15. *Cf.* also C. F. D. Moule, *op. cit.*, pp. 156ff. and especially the quotation from E. Trocmé on p. 157.

The Synoptic Gospels offer no evidence of this, not even in Peter's confession of him as the Christ, the Son of the living God (Mt. 16:16). Moule has convincingly shown, in a comparison of the Gospel of Luke and the book of Acts, 'that the author of Luke-Acts regarded the christology expressed by Jesus' own contemporaries in the pre-crucifixion ministry of Jesus as less explicit than that which was entertained after the resurrection'.[17]

For the disciples the resurrection appears to be the turning-point. Now Jesus is called '*Kyrios*' (*cf.* Acts 2:36; 4:33; 7:59; 10:36; *etc.*). The use of this title for the risen Lord must go back to the earliest period of the church, as appears from the fact that in the fifties Paul can use the Aramaic expression '*Maranatha*' ('Our Lord, come') in a letter to a Greek-speaking church (1 Cor. 16:22).[18] At the same time this expression indicates that at a very early stage Jesus was worshipped by Christians from both Jewish and Gentile backgrounds. It was certainly happening when Paul wrote his letters. Without any hesitation he speaks of his fellow-believers as 'those who call on the name of our Lord Jesus Christ' (1 Cor. 1:2). This attitude of worship may well have been the seedbed for New Testament Christology. Both R. T. France and Ralph P. Martin point to this relationship between the worshipping of Jesus and Christology. France believes that 'it was this attitude of worship which in turn found expression in the more explicit and sophisticated Christological language',[19] and Martin states 'that it was *in worship* that the decisive step was made of setting the exalted Christ on a level with God as the recipient of the church's praise'.[20]

The alternative Christologies

It is at this very point that the alternative Christologies of our day fall short. In spite of their moving personal confessions, which we have to take quite seriously, they cannot do full justice to the riches and the depth of what each of the writers of the New Testament, in his own way, says about Jesus. In all the alternative Christologies 'the continuity between New Testament Christology and the initial

---

[17] *Incarnation and Myth*, p. 136; *cf.* p. 149.
[18] *Cf.* C. F. D. Moule, *op. cit.*, p. 41, where he makes the comment: 'One does not call upon a mere Rabbi, after his death, to come.'
[19] R. T. France, *art. cit.*, p. 33.
[20] Ralph P. Martin, 'Some Reflections on New Testament Hymns', in *Christ the Lord*, p. 49.

datum in Jesus'[21] breaks down, because it has been determined beforehand that Jesus cannot be more than a man. He may be permeated fully and exhaustively by God,[22] yet he is no more than man. He may be called 'the perfected covenant man, *the* new man, the eschatological man', but in each case he does not really rise above an essentially human level. Consequently, the alternative Christologies must all 'functionalize' the Christological titles accorded to Jesus in the whole New Testament.

This is in particular true of the title 'Son of God'. All these theologians say that we should not take this title in an ontological sense, but rather see it against the background of the Old Testament, where it is an indication of the faithful covenant partner. Berkhof points out that in the Old Testament it is used of Israel as a whole and of the king. In both cases it is 'a matter of a covenantal relationship of mutual love and (with man) of obedience'.[23] He further points out that in the same sense the New Testament calls the believers children and sons of God. According to him, the term apparently did not have an exclusive meaning for Jewish ears (nor for Hellenistic ears, *cf.* the Stoa).

This interpretation, however, runs entirely contrary to what the Gospels tell us. There we read that scribes and Pharisees construed Jesus' claim of a special relationship with his heavenly Father quite differently. According to Mark 2:7 they accused Jesus of blasphemy, because he forgave the paralytic for his sins. In John 5:18 we read that 'the Jews sought all the more to kill him, because he not only broke the sabbath but also called God his Father, making himself equal with God'. Fully in line with this they later on say to Pilate: 'We have a law, and by that law he ought to die, because he has made himself the Son of God' (Jn. 19:7; *cf.* Mt. 26:65f.; Lk. 22:70).

Naturally, the advocates of alternative Christologies also reject the idea of Jesus' pre-existence. They all re-interpret the New Testament texts that speak of such a pre-existence as Jewish or Hellenistic ways of expressing that Jesus is the fruit of the divine initiative.[24] The question, however, that has to be asked here is whether such re-interpretation can really do justice to the New Testament kerygma about Jesus. Careful reading shows that both the term 'Son of God' and the concept of 'pre-existence' (the two cannot be separated!) are more than just ways of expressing the unique and universal signifi-

---

[21] C. F. D. Moule, *op. cit.*, p. 9.
[22] Hendrikus Berkhof, *The Christian Faith*, p. 287.
[23] *Ibid.*, p. 282.   [24] *Cf.* Berkhof, *op. cit.*, p. 289.

cance of Jesus in creation and redemption. They are so deeply embedded in the New Testament and stated in such an unequivocal manner that we have to take them utterly seriously. Indeed, they can be explained only in terms of 'incarnational' theology. It is really not enough when Frances Young speaks of 'incarnational elements' in the New Testament.[25] The New Testament Christology can be understood properly only in terms of a *real* incarnation.

The term 'Son of God' is not just a designation given to Jesus on the basis of his resurrection, although it is true that the resurrection marked a new stage in his manifestation as the Son of God, 'in power' (Rom. 1:4). But even before his resurrection he is called the Son of God. The New Testament speaks of his Sonship also in connection with his transfiguration (*cf.* Mt. 17:5 – 'This is my beloved Son, with whom I am well pleased'), his baptism (*cf.* Mt. 3:17 – the same words) and with his birth (*cf.* the words of Gabriel to Mary: 'the child born to you will be called holy, the Son of God', Lk. 1:35). Yes, the New Testament traces this Sonship back into all eternity. He is 'the only Son who is in the bosom of the Father' (Jn. 1:18) and shared the glory of the Father before the world was made (Jn. 17:5).

This is also the secret of all those texts that speak of his pre-existence (*cf.* Phil. 2:5ff.; Gal. 4:4; Col. 1:15–17; Heb. 1:1–3; John 1:1–3; *cf.* also all the texts in the Synoptic Gospels, according to which Jesus himself again and again says: 'I have come . . .'). It will not do to put these texts aside as Jewish or Hellenistic expressions to indicate the significance of Jesus. Again I would emphasize that nearly all these texts were written by Jews. Let us face it, the very idea of an incarnation was completely foreign to the Jewish mind. The entire Old Testament stresses the unbridgeable gulf between the transcendent God and man, a creature of flesh and blood, taken out of the ground (Gn. 3:19). And yet, here Jewish writers speak of the pre-existence of this man Jesus of Nazareth as the eternal Son and they speak of his appearance ('epiphany', *cf.* 2 Tim. 1:10) in incarnational terms. But, of course, these terms are really the only ones which can do justice to the miracle that Jesus *is*!

I. Howard Marshall rightly points out that the view that the incarnation is found merely on the fringe of the New Testament is a complete travesty of the facts.[26] We find it everywhere: in the writings of John, in the writings of Paul (including the Pastoral

[25] *The Myth of God Incarnate*, p. 19.   [26] I. Howard Marshall, *art. cit.*, p. 13.

Epistles), in the Epistle to the Hebrews and in 1 Peter. For all these writers it is the 'organizing principle of their Christology'. And it is not a matter of functionality only, but it has its ontological basis in Jesus' unique, pre-existent Sonship.

Functional versus ontological?

Nearly all alternative Christologies opt for a functional Christology over against an ontological Christology. Whatever their differences may be, they all claim that Jesus was functionally equivalent to God. Naturally, this can be worked out in different ways. William L. Schutter points out that there is an almost limitless variety of functional Christologies possible.[27] Yet they all share the same essential thrust: 'Jesus is not God; He is God's agent or representative. The more traditionally oriented the functional christology happens to be the more stress there is upon Jesus' uniqueness as agent.'

In many cases, for instance, in the Christology of Berkhof, Jesus is 'no less central or indispensable for salvation than if he were God of very God'. The greatest attraction of a functional Christology, however, lies in the fact 'that the riddle of *how a human being could simultaneously be God* can be effectively by-passed'. Summing up, Schutter says: 'Functional christologies can accommodate themselves much more easily to the question raised by the historical-critical method, the history of religions, and mythology. The paradox of how God became man is avoided, and so is the embarrassment it has caused theologians! Hence, if it becomes awkward at any point to justify the origins of ontological christology on historical grounds, then functional christology may seem to be the best alternative which sacrifices the least while preserving the most.'[28]

But can the functional and the ontological aspects really be separated? It is striking that many 'functionalists' are aware of the problems involved in such a separation. Edward Schillebeeckx, who advocates a functional Christology, nevertheless tries to bring the two aspects as closely together as possible. He affirms that Jesus is the decisive and definitive revelation of God.[29] But, of course, to say this is to have a problem on your hands. Schillebeeckx realizes this: 'We cannot separate God's nature and his revelation. Therefore in the definition of what he is, the man Jesus is indeed connected with

---

[27] William L. Schutter, 'A Continuing Crisis for Incarnational Doctrine', *The Reformed Review* 32/2, p. 84.
[28] *Ibid.*, p. 85. [29] E. Schillebeeckx, *Interim Report*, 1980, p. 142.

the nature of God'. But that is as far as he is willing to go, for he refuses to make this 'theoretically more precise'. But exactly this refusal causes him to stay within the confines of a merely functional Christology. The same is true, as we have seen,[30] of Berkhof.

A very interesting case is also the view of Cullmann. At first he strongly advocated a functional Christology. At the end of his book, *The Christology of the New Testament*, he stated: 'In the light of the New Testament witness, all mere speculation about his natures is an absurdity. Functional Christology is the only kind which exists',[31] for 'the New Testament neither is able nor intends to give information about how we are to conceive the being of God beyond the history of relevation'.[32] However, when afterwards he was attacked at this very point, he retreated and stated his agreement with Chalcedon. He even affirmed that Chalcedon 'corresponds to what the Christology of the New Testament presupposes'.[33] Yet at the same time he maintained that the reflection of Chalcedon, while an 'absolute necessity', is *not* exegesis of the New Testament. The exegete limits himself to functional Christology.

But is such a distinction, not to say separation, really tenable? G. C. Berkouwer points out that 'the [ancient] church meant to found its confession of Christ on the New Testament' and never meant 'to separate dogma from the New Testament'.[34] This does not mean that there was no development. One can indeed speak of a functional *origin* of New Testament Christology. In their reflection the first Christians started with what Christ had done for them, or perhaps we should say: what God had done to Jesus Christ and therefore to them. In their early liturgy and confessions they tried to express that in Jesus Christ they had discovered a new reality of salvation. But from the very start this was connected with the *person* of Christ.

In the early liturgy and confessions we already hear who he *is*. To the ancient church the dilemma articulated by Bultmann, 'Does he help me because he is God's Son, or is he the Son of God because he helps me?',[35] would have been altogether incomprehensible. R. H. Fuller is unquestionably right when he says that 'it is not just a quirk of the Greek mind, but a universal human apperception, that action implies prior being – even if, as is also true, being is only

---

[30] See pp. 75f., above.   [31] *Op. cit.*, p. 326.   [32] *Ibid.*, p. 327.
[33] *Cf.* 'The Reply of Prof. Cullmann to Roman Catholic Critics', *Scottish Journal of Theology*, 1962, pp. 36ff.
[34] G. C. Berkouwer, *A Half Century of Theology*, 1977, p. 233.
[35] Rudolf Bultmann, *Essays*, 1955, p. 280.

apprehended in action'.[36] In other words, functional and ontological approaches are complementary.[37]

'From below' or 'from above'?

The same is true, we believe, of the distinction between a Christology 'from below' and one 'from above'. Actually, the idea of a Christology 'from below' is not new at all. Luther, for instance, more than once emphasized that the biblical account starts with the humanity of Jesus and only gradually discloses his messiahship and deity. 'The Scriptures begin very gently, and lead us on to Christ as to a man, and then to one who is Lord over all creatures, and after that to one who is God. So do I enter delightfully and learn to know God. But the philosophers and doctors have insisted on beginning from above. We must begin from below, and after that come upwards.'[38] Somewhere else he opposes the Sophists, who pictured Christ by mixing his two natures in a curious way, and replies: 'Christ is not called Christ because He had two natures. What has that fact to do with me? He bears His glorious and comforting name because of His work and office; what He did provides Him with the name.'[39] Yet this approach did not prevent Luther from accepting the formula of Chalcedon without any hesitation. In fact, he strictly adhered to the idea of our Lord having the divine and the human nature in the unity of the divine Person.

It is exactly at this point that we encounter the problem of the new Christologies. In the case of Berkhof, it is even a *double* problem, because he opts for a twofold historical approach: (i) 'from behind' – we see him in the line of redemptive history, how he arises out of the Old Testament impasse to provide and to be the answer to it; (ii) 'from below' – we see what he looks like in the light of a careful investigation of the sources and within the framework of his own time.[40]

As far as the first approach is concerned, we must begin with a word of appreciation. In the past, dogmatics often proceeded directly from the doctrines of creation, man and sin to the doctrine of Christ. God's dealing with Israel did not receive special attention, even though the Old Testament precedes the New. By introducing a

---

[36] R. H. Fuller, *op. cit.*, p. 248.
[37] *Cf.* R. T. France, *art. cit.*, pp. 33f.
[38] Martin Luther, *Werke EA* (Erlanger Ausgabe) 12, p. 412.
[39] *EA* 25, pp. 207f.   [40] Hendrikus Berkhof, *op. cit.*, p. 267.

special chapter on 'Israel',[41] Berkhof correctly draws our attention to the redemptive-historical character of God's work of salvation.

But the question is how such a chapter functions within the totality of our dogmatics. Is it the prelude to the actual saving event still to come, namely, God's redemptive work in Jesus Christ, or is it the determinative hermeneutical key for our understanding of Jesus Christ? Is Jesus the fulfilment of Israel's history, providing the final clue for the understanding of this history, or is what happens in him only the final act of the history of Israel, the consequence being that this history determines who Jesus is? Berkhof prefers the latter approach, as appears from the following statement: 'The Old Testament, John the Baptist, his passion and death, his resurrection, his new mode of existence as the living Lord – everything is joined together in the one continuous covenantal way of God with his people, on which Jesus Christ turns out to be God's great and definitive step toward his future and to us.'[42]

As far as the second approach is concerned, the approach 'from below', we must again start with a word of appreciation. Luther was certainly right when he said that this is the way the Bible itself leads us to the secret of who Jesus is: from Jesus as a man to Christ as Lord and God. But this, of course, is quite different from what modern theologians understand by 'from below'. For them, this is a strictly historical approach, by which the present-day investigator tries to bore through the layers of post-Easter interpretations in order to discover the 'real' Jesus.

But is this still possible after the resurrection? As we have seen before, and as is also admitted by Berkhof,[43] the oldest documents in the New Testament all look at Jesus from the perspective of the resurrection. By the resurrection (and the subsequent gift of the Spirit) the secret of Jesus' life has been revealed, and from now on the church can see him only in this light. The approach 'from above' is now indispensable and final. That does not mean that there is no place left for the approaches 'from before' and 'from below'. In fact, they are included in the approach 'from above'. Marshall summarizes his own study of the origins of New Testament Christology as follows:

---

[41] *Ibid.*, pp. 221–265.   [42] *Ibid.*, p. 280.
[43] *Cf. Ibid.*, p. 273: 'We cannot point to a time, however brief, when it [the picture of the historical Jesus in the Synoptic Gospels] functioned without the image of the exalted Christ.'

The evidence supports the view that it was the resurrection of Jesus which gave the decisive stimulus to Christological thinking . . . The earliest Christology stressed the way in which he fulfilled the Old Testament promises of a coming deliverer. It saw in Jesus the agent of God entrusted with the power to save and to judge, and it confessed him as the Lord to whom was given absolute authority. From these statements it was a short step to the application to him of the same authority and nature as God, and to the realization that, in whatever weak sense these traits might be seen in other messengers of God, he possessed them in a unique way as the Son of God.[44]

It is no wonder that many theologians reject the dilemma 'from below'/'from above' as a *false dilemma*. Jürgen Moltmann asserts that the difference between the two approaches is 'only apparent',[45] and Martin Hengel calls it 'a false alternative that goes against the course of New Testament christology, which develops in an indissoluble dialectic between God's saving activity and man's answer'.[46]

Wherever we start, the result will always be that in the course of our investigation we are compelled to speak about Jesus '*with two words*'. It may indeed be preferable in our time to start with the concrete historical figure of Jesus of Nazareth, as he comes to us from the pages of the Synoptic Gospels. But even then we cannot help discovering two things: (i) this Jesus of Nazareth is the Christ in whom the writers, belonging to the post-resurrection church, believed; (ii) this Jesus simply does not fit into our ordinary earthly categories, as appears from both his words and his deeds.

All who start 'from below' encounter this remarkable, incomprehensible fact. We see this in the Christologies of Schoonenberg, Schillebeeckx, Küng, Robinson, Berkhof. All have to admit that we need 'two sets of language, man-language and God-language',[47] if we want to do justice to Jesus. But everything depends on *how* we use these two sets of language. Robinson chooses to apply them to the *man* Jesus. 'The formula we presuppose is not of one superhuman person with two natures, divine and human, but of one human person of whom we must use two languages, man-language

[44] I. Howard Marshall, *The Origins of New Testament Christology*, p. 128.
[45] Jürgen Moltmann, *The Crucified God*, 1974, p. 91.
[46] Martin Hengel, *The Son of God*, 1976, p. 92.
[47] J. A. T. Robinson, *The Human Face of God*, 1973, p. 116.

and God-language. Jesus is wholly and completely a man, but a man who "speaks true" not simply of humanity but of God.'[48] All the other advocates of an alternative Christology virtually make the same choice.

The New Testament writers made a different choice. True, they all believe that Jesus was a real man. But at the same time they all believe that he simultaneously and uniquely stands *on the side of God*. 'This uniqueness is no less a reality than his being a true man.'[49] When for instance the writer of the Fourth Gospel wants to express the glory of the earthly Jesus, 'he cannot speak of this glory in any other way but in divine categories, because his glory exceeds everything that preceded him in history, even the glory of Moses'.[50] This way of speaking about Jesus is characteristic of the whole New Testament and it is no wonder that within this context we soon see the rise of ideas of *pre-existence* and *incarnation*. These ideas are not put upon the earthly Jesus as additional but essentially foreign elements, but they are derived from the secret of his person as revealed in the resurrection. In fact, the incarnation of the pre-existent Son of God is the only possibility to express the secret of this man. He not only was on the side of God; *he came from God and was himself God*.

[48] *Ibid.*, p. 113.
[49] A. van de Beek, *De menselijke persoon van Christus*, 1980, p. 196.
[50] Herman Ridderbos, *Studies in Scripture and its Authority*, 1978, p. 68.

Chapter Nine

Chalcedon, ontology and salvation

It was this mystery of the incarnation of the pre-existent Son of God that the Fathers of the ancient church wanted to safeguard over against all kinds of attempts of their day to make the Christian gospel more understandable or more acceptable, by downgrading either Jesus' humanity or his divinity. Therefore Nicea spoke of the man Jesus of Nazareth as *vere Deus* AND *vere homo*. They were well aware of the fact that they could not make the mystery of his being transparent. They did not try to do this either, not even in the definition of Chalcedon. Admittedly, it was a rather complicated formula that went beyond the mere statement of the *vere Deus* and the *vere homo*.

It also tried to say something about the relationship between the divinity and the humanity of Christ. It had to do this, because there were views abroad which did injustice to either of the two aspects or to both of them. The Antiochene school, as represented by Nestorius, did injustice to the unity by tending to distinguish a divine and a human person in the one Christ. The Alexandrian school, as represented by Eutyches, did injustice to the true humanity by at least giving the impression that after the incarnation there was only one nature in which the humanity of Christ was actually swallowed up in his deity. Hence the repeated emphasis on the unity of Christ: 'one and the same Son', 'one and the same Christ', and on the two natures. Hence also the famous four negatives: '*without* confusion, *without* change, *without* division, *without* separation'. By these four negatives, the so-called *alpha privantia*, the Fathers set up 'a double row of light-beacons which mark off the navigable water in between and warn against the dangers which threaten to the left and to the right'.[1]

At the same time the Council also wanted to do as much justice

[1] G. C. Berkouwer, *The Person of Christ*, 1954, p. 85.

as possible to the various schools of thought that were in existence at the time. For this reason Chalcedon has been called one of the most truly ecumenical councils in the entire history of the church. Aloys Grillmeier says that in this formula 'as in almost no other formula from the early councils, all the important centres of Church life and all the trends of contemporary theology, Rome, Alexandria, Constantinople and Antioch, have contributed toward the framing of a common expression of faith'.[2] It may be helpful to quote the central part of the formula in full.

> We all with one voice confess our Lord Jesus Christ, one and the same Son, the same perfect in Godhead, the same perfect in manhood, very God and very man, the same consisting of a reasonable soul and a body, of one substance (*homo-ousion*) with the Father as touching the Godhead, the same of one substance with us as touching the manhood, like us in all things, sin except; begotten of the Father before the worlds as touching the Godhead, the same in these last days, for us and for our salvation, born of the Virgin Mary, the Mother of God, as touching the manhood, one and the same Christ, Son, Lord, Only-begotten, to be acknowledged of two natures (*en duo physesin*) without confusion, without change, without division, without separation (*asynchytos, atreptos, adiairetos, achoristos*); the distinction of natures being in no wise done away because of the union, but rather the characteristic property of each nature being preserved, and concurring into one Person and one subsistence (*eis hen prosopon kai mian hypostasin*), not as if Christ were parted or divided into two Persons, but one and the same Son and Only-begotten God, Word, Lord, Jesus Christ.[3]

Ontological categories

It is evident that the Fathers expressed their view in terms and concepts of that particular period. Terms such as *ousia* (substance, being), *physis* (nature), *prosopon* (person), *hypostasis* (subsistence) belonged to the common Hellenistic vocabulary of that time. In the nineteenth century Adolf von Harnack voiced his opinion that these

[2] Aloys Grillmeier, *Christ in Christian Tradition*, 1975, p. 555.
[3] Text (with a few minor changes) taken from R. V. Sellers, *The Council of Chalcedon*, 1961, p. 203.

Hellenistic thought-forms had distorted the original gospel. Very few scholars of today, however, would be willing to say with him that 'dogma in its conception and development is a work of the Greek spirit on the soil of the gospel'.[4] It is generally acknowledged that, even though Hellenistic terms and concepts were used, the resulting Christology was very un-Hellenistic. John Macquarrie is altogether right when he says: 'Christian doctrines were not conformed to the mould of already existing terminologies, but terms already available were adopted into Christian discourse and given new meanings.'[5]

This is not to deny that the formulations used by the Council are very difficult for us today, and that for several reasons. First, the terms do not have an unequivocal meaning. In fact, already at the time of Chalcedon itself the terms had different meanings. This is in particular true of the words *ousia*, *physis* and *hypostasis*. They not only varied but also overlapped.[6] Macquarrie goes even so far as to say: 'Each of these three terms could and did have at least three distinct meanings, and any one of the three terms could and sometimes did bear any one of the three meanings' (namely, substance, essence, subsistence).[7] Yet it is not impossible to obtain a fairly good idea of what the Fathers of the Council meant by the terms.

1. *Ousia* is an indication of 'substance'. The term had already played an important role in the development of Trinitarian theology. For the Fathers *ousia* was, metaphorically speaking, 'the particular slab of material stuff which constitutes a given object'.[8] Applied to the three Persons of the Trinity it means: the same stuff or substance of deity has three different representations or, conversely, each Person possesses the same and the complete stuff or substance of deity. Applied to the *homo-ousios* as used of Christ in the formula of Chalcedon it means: he possesses the complete stuff or substance of deity and the complete stuff or substance of humanity.

2. *Physis* is an indication of the sum-total of 'basic properties that makes something one thing rather than another'.[9] Applied to Christ in the formula of Chalcedon it means: he possesses all the properties that make God God and all the properties that make man man.

[4] Adolf von Harnack, *The History of Dogma*, 1894, p. 17.
[5] John Macquarrie, 'The Chalcedonian Definition', *The Expository Times*, December 1972, p. 72.
[6] *Ibid.*, p. 69.
[7] *Ibid.*, pp. 69f.
[8] G. L. Prestige, *God in Patristic Thought*, (1952) 1964, p. 168.
[9] Macquarrie, *art. cit.*, p. 70.

3. *Hypostasis* is perhaps the most difficult term of all. Etymologically it means: that which underlies or that which gives support. Throughout the centuries it was used in a variety of ways,[10] but gradually it obtained the meaning of a 'positive and concrete and distinct existence, first of all in the abstract, and later . . . in the particular individual'.[11] In this way it came very near in meaning to the term *prosōpon*, which stands for 'individual'.[12] In the formula both terms are used side by side: 'concurring into one Person (*prosōpon*) and one subsistence (*hypostasis*)'. Both are indicative of the 'bearer' and (in this case, too) of the principle of unity of the natures.

A second problem posed by Chalcedon to people of today is that some of the terms have taken on different meanings in the course of the centuries. For instance, today the term 'person' belongs to the psychological rather than the ontological order of things. Using this term today we are inclined to think of personality, of the psychological qualities of a man or woman. In the climate of Chalcedon 'person' had an ontological meaning, indicating the subject behind all those psychological phenomena. Hence Chalcedon can speak of the Logos as the one Person who is the subject of both his divine and his human qualities.

A third problem, perhaps the most vexing for people of today, is that, because of its ontological and philosophical terminology and nature, the language of Chalcedon sounds abstruse and even unreal. Modern man is unable to discover the living Lord in this kind of language. He whose mysterious being is described in this formula seems to be an abstraction rather than a living person. How different is this description from the picture offered to us by the Gospels! There we see a living man whose words and deeds are vibrant with life and power! The Chalcedonian formula does not seem to be even a pale copy of this picture.

However, we should not make the mistake of attributing to the Fathers of the Council intentions which they never had. For them the discussions preceding Chalcedon and coming to a head at the Council itself were very live and existential issues. They were not discussing a merely theological problem in the manner in which philosophers debate a philosophical point; their deepest concern was the reality of our redemption by God. At the Council of Nicea the

---

[10] *Cf.* Prestige, *op. cit.*, p. 63.   [11] *Ibid.*, p. 174.

[12] Prestige indicates the difference as follows: 'prosopon was a non-metaphysical term for "individual", while hypostasis was a more or less metaphysical term for "independent object" ', *op. cit.*, p. 179.

church had confessed that Jesus Christ was the Son of God who is of one substance (*homo-ousios*) with the Father. But this was not the whole truth about the mystery of redemption. If the Son came to us from the Father, did he really enter into our human life? If so, how can these two aspects of his life be reconciled?

These difficult questions vexed the church between Nicea (325) and Chalcedon (451) and Chalcedon was the final attempt to arrive at a common understanding. Whatever one may think of the terminology used, it cannot be denied that Chalcedon achieved two things: (i) it established a norm of doctrine in a field in which there had been great confusion; (ii) it did justice to the fundamental conviction of the church that in Christ a complete revelation of God is made in terms of a genuine human life.[13]

Does this mean that Chalcedon is the last word, that it is a 'terminal point', beyond which the church cannot proceed? More than once this has been asserted,[14] but we believe that such a view is not correct. For one thing, it forgets that the witness of Scripture to Jesus Christ is so rich and so profound that it cannot possibly be exhausted by any one dogmatical formulation. For another, it also forgets the limited nature of the definition of Chalcedon. As the French theologian, Jean Galot, points out, 'the Chalcedonian formula of faith does not go into explanations of what nature is or what person or hypostasis is. It does not even concern itself with defining the act of the Incarnation, but limits itself to declaring what exists in Christ. It does not specify the relationship between Christ's ontological constitution and his redemptive mission, but limits itself to a general affirmation: "For us and for our salvation" '.[15] What is abundantly clear, however, is the fact that the church believed that the mystery of Christ's coming can be expressed only in incarnational terms.

The incarnation

It cannot be denied that the term 'incarnation' is very difficult and by no means immediately transparent. As a matter of fact, in the course of the last centuries there have been many different interpretations.[16] In this section, however, we are concerned with the

[13] *Cf.* Williston Walker, *A History of the Christian Church*, (1918) 1976, p. 139.
[14] *Cf.* G. C. Berkouwer, *op. cit.*, pp. 85ff.
[15] Jean Galot S. J., *Who is Christ? A Theology of the Incarnation*, 1981, p. 249.
[16] *Cf.* Brian Hebblethwaite, 'The propriety of the doctrine of the Incarnation as a way of interpreting Christ', in *Scottish Journal of Theology* 33, June 1980, pp. 201f.

'classical' interpretation, which can be defined as 'God's self-revelation here on earth, not only in but as the man Jesus of Nazareth', or as 'the unique and unrepeatable act of God, in one of the modes of his being, in coming amongst us, living a human life and dying a human death'.[17] This is what the ancient church wanted to express when it spoke of the *vere Deus* and the *vere homo* at the same time.

As we have seen, this very same idea of speaking of one who is both God and man has increasingly come under attack. One of the main points of criticism is that it would lack inner coherence. 'Speaking of God *being* part of his own creation or a part of that creation *being* God . . . involves a logical contradiction.'[18] In reply to this criticism orthodox theology has often appealed to the incomprehensibility of God and to the mysterious nature of God's unique act in Jesus Christ. Undoubtedly such an appeal is fully legitimate, but at the same time we must admit that it is not enough. It is also necessary to adduce 'positive grounds' for thinking that it is conceivable that God, the Creator of the universe, including man himself, is able to live out a human life to the full, without ceasing to be God.[19] In order to do this we have to move in at least three directions.

First of all, we have to spell out the Trinitarian nature of God. Only when there is a fullness of personal relations within the Godhead itself is it conceivable that 'God can live out a human life from a centre in himself, and relate himself to himself in the manner in which we read of the prayers of Jesus to the Father'.[20]

Secondly, we have to reflect more deeply on what this assumption of a full human life by God means for the relation of the deity and the humanity in Christ. If we take the deity seriously, does this not mean that actually nothing is really added to the Son, because as God he already knows humanity to the full? Is God not perfect in his innermost being and does perfection, if taken seriously, not mean that nothing can be added to it? Jean Galot's reply to these questions is that we indeed may not in any way subtract from the divine perfection. It is true that the Son's human life cannot add any perfection to his perfect being as God. At the same time we should realize that the human existence provided the Son with an irreplace-

---

[17] *Ibid.*, p. 202.

[18] Maurice Wiles in *Incarnation and Myth* (ed. Michael Goulder), 1979, p. 6.

[19] *Cf.* Hebblethwaite, *art. cit.*, pp. 212f.

[20] *Ibid.*, p. 213. *Cf.* also D. M. MacKinnon, 'The Relation of the Doctrines of the Incarnation and the Trinity', in Richard W. A. McKinney (ed.), *Creation, Christ and Culture, Studies in Honour of T. F. Torrance*, 1976, pp. 92–107, esp. pp. 99f.

able experience. 'Divine knowledge of human realities cannot be identified with man's personal experience of them. It was precisely this experience that enabled the Son of God to know the human universe in a different way than before.'[21] This also means that there is no reason whatever to subtract from the full humanity of Christ. He really and 'integrally experienced the life of man, under the same conditions as all other humans'.[22] He lacked nothing that was human. He had a truly human mind, will, consciousness and personality. His birth, his life, his suffering, his death, they were all truly human in the full sense of the word.

Thirdly, we must further explore what it means that the *person* of the Saviour, that is, the subject of his human life, was the eternal Son of God. This aspect in particular has for many people been the great stumbling-block against accepting the classical Christology of Chalcedon. Does the exclusion of the human person as the subject of his human life not mean that we unavoidably arrive at some form of docetism? Is personhood not essential to full humanity? We must admit that these questions are very much to the point and have to be taken very seriously. Even though in the incarnation we are dealing with a unique mystery, we have no right to avoid troubling questions but must face them honestly in order to do full justice to the humanity of the Saviour, no less than to his divinity.

Personally we find the thinking of Jean Galot very helpful here. He points out that in common parlance we do not distinguish between person and nature, but usually mean by person the whole being, *i.e.* the person together with the nature he possesses.[23] In Christology, however, such a distinction is necessary, and psychologically it is possible too. In psychological experience we discover that 'the person is discovered essentially in our relations with others'. I become aware of myself by knowing an object outside myself. I discover myself as an 'I' only when I am confronted with another person, that is, with a 'you', in a face-to-face contact. In this contact I discover that my 'I' that meets the other is always the same. My 'I' possesses 'an originality that makes it unique, different from all other "I's" '.[24]

All this means that the formal constituent of human being is found in 'relational being'.[25] Naturally, this sounds very abstract and may even seem to be unreal. Is a human person not much more? Does

[21] Galot, *op. cit.*, p. 273.   [22] *Ibid.*, p. 273.   [23] *Ibid.*, p. 293.
[24] *Ibid.*, p. 297.   [25] *Ibid.*, p. 293.

he not possess an individual human nature (including intellect and will) as well? Galot does not deny this, but he does maintain that if one tries to distinguish what belongs strictly to the nature and what to the person, one must conclude that person in the strict sense can be defined only as a relational being.

Applied to the incarnation, this means: 'Jesus' human nature is fully endowed with human reality and human existence . . . In particular, he has a human soul with a human consciousness and a human will, a soul that acts according to the laws of human psychology and remains distinct from his divine spirit, "without any commingling". Without losing any of its own qualities, this human nature is personalized by the relational being of the Word. Jesus' human activity is not governed by a human "I", but by the "I" of the Son of God which inspires and guides it. That is why the man Jesus possesses a completely filial personality, capable of enhancing in the most complete way all that is human about him.'[26] At the same time, 'in becoming man, the relational being of the Son inaugurated horizontal relationships with men. His contacts were no longer directed solely downward from above. They were henceforth to be made on a level of equality with human nature. Through this human nature a divine relational being entered into human interpersonal relations'.[27]

Does all this mean that we have now 'explained' the mystery? Definitely not! It is only an attempt to unfold in more modern language what Chalcedon tried to say in the terminology of its own time. The incarnation itself remains a mystery that can never be 'explained'. All we can do is to 'describe' it by listening carefully to the witness of Scripture and by expounding what this witness in a great variety of approaches communicates to us. But even in this exposition the mystery itself remains fully inexplicable, for the heart of the mystery is that the eternal Son of God was willing to enter into a fully human existence. What is even more, the Son of God in this human existence became a servant and became obedient unto death, even death on a cross (Phil. 2:8).

This unfathomable mystery the Fathers of Chalcedon wanted to safeguard. Their ontological approach, taken in isolation, may seem to be very static, but behind all the 'static' formulations there is a dynamic conception. Their real concern was to safeguard the message of the prologue of John's Gospel: the Word that was in the begin-

[26] *Ibid.*, p. 306.   [27] *Ibid.*, p. 307.

ning, that was with God, yes, that was God, became flesh and dwelt among us (Jn. 1:1, 14).

Any tampering with this mystery always has far-reaching consequences for the rest of our theology. In the chapters on the alternative Christologies we have already seen that moving away from Chalcedon directly affects the doctrine of the Trinity. If Jesus is only 'true man', then there is no place left for the idea that God is triune in his innermost being. At the most one can speak of an 'economic' Trinity or a 'Trinity-in-revelation', but one can no longer speak of an 'essential' or 'ontological' Trinity.

But the consequences are not limited to the doctrine of the Trinity. In his review of *The Myth of God Incarnate*, John Macquarrie comments: 'Christian doctrines are so closely interrelated that if you take away one, several others tend to collapse. After incarnation is thrown out, is the doctrine of the Trinity bound to go? What kind of doctrine of atonement remains possible? Would the Eucharist be reduced simply to a memorial service? What a rewriting of creeds and liturgies, of prayer books and hymn books, even of Holy Scripture, would be demanded!'[28]

The authority of Scripture

The last words of this quotation point to the real crux of the matter. Those who advocate an alternative Christology hold a different view of Scripture from the Fathers of Chalcedon. Undoubtedly the advocates of an alternative Christology also regard Scripture as indispensable; yet in the final analysis it is no more than a human witness. It is the attempt of the early church to express in human words what they have seen in Jesus; in the words of Robert L. Wilken: 'The value of the New Testament witness is not that it definitely states the truth about Christianity, but that it bears witness to the earliest experience of Christianity that we possess.'[29] Because here we have the witness to the earliest experience, we have to listen carefully and attentively to this witness, but ultimately it is our duty to state in our own words what we in our own day see in Jesus. In his lecture to the European Division of the World Alliance of Reformed Churches, Berkhof put it thus: The early church in Palestine wrestled with the question of who Jesus is. In the New Testament

---

[28] *The Truth of God Incarnate*, p. 144.
[29] Robert L. Wilken, *The Myth of Christian Beginnings*, 1979, p. 171.

we see that they attributed many titles to Jesus: Son of man, Messiah, Son of God, Word, Lord, and others. But none of these titles can say everything. Jesus does not offer a Christology; he offers himself. And he invites *us* to seek the name by which *we* can confess what he means to *us*.[30]

Schillebeeckx writes in similar vein in his *Interim Report*. First he states what the New Testament is about. In this collection of writings we are confronted with a basic experience: 'Jesus, experienced as the decisive and definitive saving event; salvation from God, Israel's age-old dream'.[31] 'But precisely because it is a matter of experience, these authors express this salvation in terms of the world in which they live, their own milieu and their own questionings – in short, in terms of their own world of experience.' Obviously, our world of experience is quite different from theirs, but we need not worry about this. As the writers of the New Testament felt free to talk of the experience of salvation in Jesus in a variety of ways, so we too have the freedom to express in new forms the experience of salvation in Jesus that we may have and to describe it in terms taken from our modern culture with its own particular problems, expectations and needs.[32] In fact, this is the only way for us to remain faithful to what the New Testament Christians felt to be an experience of salvation in Jesus. To say the same we must say it differently!

We do not deny that there is an important element of truth in the approach of both Berkhof and Schillebeeckx. Indeed, it is the duty of today's church to say in words and categories of our own day what Jesus means to us. But this is only one side of the truth. There is also the other side, which in our opinion remains obscured in this approach. It is the question: What is the authority of the apostolic witness in this re-interpretation of Jesus and his work in words and categories of our own day and age? Is it normative? Are we bound by it, so that we are not allowed to deviate from it? Or does the New Testament give us only some general directions, leaving it to us to make our own decisions?

At the back of this there is still another question. Whence did the New Testament writers derive their own interpretation? Was it only an expression of their own personal, subjective experience of the risen Lord? Or does this interpretation actually go back to the self-interpretation of Jesus during his life on earth? I know there is

[30] Hendrikus Berkhof, *The Reformed World*, art. cit., p. 298.
[31] Edward Schillebeeckx, *Interim Report*, 1980, p. 15.
[32] Cf. *Ibid.*, p. 16.

much difference of opinion among New Testament scholars as to Jesus' own self-consciousness and self-interpretation. Yet even the 'minimalists' admit that Jesus was aware of his special, even unique place in the history of Israel and of his special, unique relationship with God.

The question is this: Can we do justice to this self-awareness of Jesus, if we explain it in functional categories only? Or does it have an ontological basis as well? Were such New Testament writers as Paul and John and the author of Hebrews actually trespassing, when they spoke of Jesus in terms that were *both* functional *and* ontological? Did they, in doing this, attribute to him more than was really justified? H. M. Kuitert puts the problem thus: 'The real issue is: is the significance of Jesus given to Him or received from Him?'[33] His own answer is: 'The interpretation of Jesus, His way, and His work as the way of salvation . . . comes from Jesus Himself. This is a dogmatic assertion. Exegesis has the task of establishing and refining it, and it is able to do this job. Paul did not damage what Jesus accomplished. In his own way – and his way is different from that of John or the writer of Hebrews, and is more explicit than that of Jesus Himself – Paul illuminated Jesus in His person and work by means of the person and work itself.' I believe that here we are at the heart of the problem.

Christology and soteriology

It is not just a theoretical problem. The ancient church fought the Christological battle because it believed that the gospel itself was at stake. I fully agree with this. The divinity of Jesus is not a dispensable 'extra' that has no real significance for our salvation. On the contrary, our salvation depends upon it. *We can be saved only by God himself.*

Many Church Fathers repeat this again and again in their works, and the same idea is encountered in the works of the Reformers. Some of the Reformation confessions state it quite bluntly. The Lutheran *Formula of Concord* quotes Luther's treatise *Concerning the Councils and the Church*: 'We Christians must know that unless God is in the balance and throws in weight as counterbalance, we shall sink to the bottom with our scale. I mean that this way: If it is not true that God died for us, but only a man died, we are lost.

[33] H. M. Kuitert, *The Reality of Faith*, 1968, p. 166.

But if God's death and God dead lie in the opposite scale, then his side goes down and we go upward like a light and empty pan. Of course, he can also go up again or jump out of his pan. But he could never have sat in the pan unless he had become a man like us, so that it could be said: God dead, God's passion, God's blood, God's death. According to his nature God cannot die, but since God and man are united in one person, it is correct to talk about God's death when that man dies who is one thing or one person with God'.[34]

The Reformed *Heidelberg Catechism*, in more sober language, says the same. First it states that the mediator and deliverer we need must be 'one who is a true and righteous man, and yet more powerful than all creatures, that is, one who at the same time is true God'. The Catechism then asks: 'Why must he at the same time be true God?' The answer is: 'So that by the power of his divinity he might bear as a man [or, as another translation has it, in his human nature] the burden of God's wrath, and recover for us and restore to us righteousness and life.'[35]

In more recent time the same has been forcefully restated by Karl Barth, who speaks of the 'exchange', the 'substitution, which God has proposed between the world and Himself present and active in the person of Jesus Christ'.[36] In Jesus Christ, God himself takes the enmity of the world against himself upon himself, making his own the situation into which it has fallen. Later on he defines the same 'exchange' as follows: 'What took place is that the Son of God fulfilled the righteous judgment on us men by Himself taking our place as man and in our place undergoing the judgment under which we had passed . . . *Cur Deus homo?* In order that God as man might do and accomplish and achieve and complete all this for us wrong-doers, in order that in this way there might be brought about by Him our reconciliation with Him and conversion to Him.'[37]

Now I do not deny that the majority of the advocates of the alternative Christologies see Jesus also as their Saviour and Redeemer. Schillebeeckx, for instance, asserts that one is a Christian, if one is convinced that final salvation-from-God is disclosed in the person of Jesus.[38] Berkhof states: 'The whole of salvation as it is comprehended in Jesus can be summed up with such words as cross,

---

[34] Cf. *The Book of Concord. The Confessions of the Evangelical Lutheran Church*, tr. Theodore G. Tappert, 1959, p. 599.

[35] Cf. *Reformed Confessions of the Sixteenth Century*, ed. Arthur Cochrane, 1966, p. 307.

[36] Karl Barth, *CD* IV, 1, p. 75. [37] *Ibid.*, pp. 222f.

[38] Edward Schillebeeckx, *Jesus*, 1979, p. 30.

suffering, dying, death, blood (that is, surrender of life). Therein the mediator identifies himself to the limit with his and God's enemies, takes all the guilt upon himself and bears it away, and as the substitute on behalf of and for man he erases it completely.'[39]

There are no traces here, especially in the case of Berkhof, of the superficial moralism of the older liberal theology, which regarded Jesus only as a great teacher and example.[40] Yet I also believe that this new Christology moves in a direction that can easily lead, perhaps even *is bound to lead*, to such deviations. If Jesus is no longer seen as the eternal Son of God, who 'for us men and for our salvation came down from heaven . . . and was made man' (Nicene Creed), if he is only the 'true man' who is the Pioneer and Forerunner, then the deepest safeguards against a moralistic transformation of the gospel have been removed. It is striking that in the affirmative confession (*homologia*) with which Schillebeeckx ends his second large volume, there is no word about the atonement. In the 'Creed' we only read:

> We nailed him to the cross.
> And he died and was buried.
> But he trusted in God's final word,
> and is risen, once and for all.[41]

And in the 'Eucharistic thanksgiving' we read:

> We recall that
> he went to search for all who were lost,
> for those who are saddened and out in the cold,
> and how he always took their side,
> without forgetting the others.

> And that cost him his life,
> because the mighty of the earth would not tolerate it.
> And yet, good God, almighty Father,
> he knew that he was understood and accepted by you,
> he saw himself confirmed by you in love.

---

[39] Hendrikus Berkhof, *The Christian Faith*, p. 303.
[40] Unfortunately the same cannot be said of most of the contributors to the volume *The Myth of God Incarnate*. Cf. the critique of Charles Moule, in *Incarnation and Myth*, p. 139.
[41] Edward Schillebeeckx, *Christ*, 1979, p. 847.

113

So he became one with you.
And so, free from himself,
he could live a life of liberation for others.[42]

Further on in the same prayer he says about the Spirit:

So send your Spirit upon us
and upon these good gifts, the good Spirit
from you and your Son, that it may inspire us
when we continue to follow Jesus:
Jesus, from whom we have learnt to be free:
free from powers which estrange us,
free to do good.[43]

If it is true that a person's real theology comes out in his liturgical creed and prayers, then we must conclude that Schillebeeckx' doctrine of atonement is seriously defective. For here is no trace of the 'exchange', which is so characteristic of the biblical doctrine of the atonement. One cannot help wondering whether it is not the result of a Christology which is equally defective, because it does not acknowledge that the eternal Son of God became man for us and for our salvation.

The seriousness of the situation should not be underestimated. John Macquarrie may be right when he says that 'it would be an anachronism to describe the positions of this book [*The Myth of God Incarnate*] as Arian, deist or Unitarian', but he is certainly right when he adds: 'Unquestionably there are affinities'.[44] Similar affinities, especially in the form of neo-Arianism, can also be detected in the case of the alternative Christologies. Indeed, there are clear indications that the Christological battle of the ancient church needs to be fought all over again.

Once again the church is faced with the question: 'Who do you say that I am?' Once again the church is being confronted by a challenge which threatens its very existence. Today, just as much as in the fourth and fifth centuries, our salvation depends upon the answer given to this fundamental question. For according to the New Testament, our salvation is nothing less than this: 'The grace of our Lord Jesus Christ who, though he was rich, yet for your sake

---

[42] *Ibid.*, p. 849.   [43] *Ibid.*, p. 850.
[44] John Macquarrie in *The Truth of God Incarnate*, p. 144.

became poor, so that by his poverty you might become rich' (2 Cor. 8:9). These words, which show no trace of mythological speculation, contain in a nutshell the whole Christology of the New Testament. And it was this very Christology that was upheld by the church both at Nicea and at Chalcedon.

Bibliography

Althaus, P., *The Theology of Martin Luther* (Fortress Press, 1966).
Anderson, J. N. D., *The Mystery of the Incarnation* (Hodder, 1978).
Barrett, C. K., *Jesus and the Gospel Tradition* (SPCK, 1967).
Barth, K., *Dogmatics in Outline* (SCM, 1949).
— *Church Dogmatics* I, 1: *The Doctrine of the Word of God*, Part 1 (T. & T. Clark, 1936).
— *Church Dogmatics* I, 2: *The Doctrine of the Word of God*, Part 2 (T. & T. Clark, 1956).
— *Church Dogmatics* IV, 1: *The Doctrine of Reconciliation*, Part 1 (T. & T. Clark, 1956).
— *Church Dogmatics* IV, 2: *The Doctrine of Reconciliation*, Part 2 (T. & T. Clark, 1961).
— *Anselm: Fides Quaerens Intellectum* (SCM, 1960).
— *The Humanity of God* (John Knox Press, 1960).
— *Evangelical Theology: An Introduction* (T. & T. Clark, 1963).
Beek, A. van de, *De menselijke persoon van Christus* (Callenbach, 1980).
Berkouwer, G. C., *The Person of Christ* (Eerdmans, 1954).
— *The Triumph of Grace in the Theology of Karl Barth* (Paternoster, 1956).
— *A Half Century of Theology* (Eerdmans, 1977).
Berkhof, H., *The Christian Faith* (Eerdmans, 1979).
Berkhof, L., *Systematic Theology* (Banner of Truth, 1959).
Birch, C., *Nature and God* (SCM, 1965).
Bray, G., *Creeds, Councils and Christ* (IVP, 1984).
Bultmann, R., *Jesus and the Word* (Nicholson & Watson, 1935).
— *Theology of the New Testament* 1 (SCM, 1952).
— 'New Testament and Mythology' in H. W. Bartsch (ed.), *Kerygma and Myth* 1 (SPCK, 1953, [5]1966).
— *Essays* (SCM, 1955).
— *Glauben und Verstehen* 1 (J. C. B. Mohr, 1964).
Carey, G., *God Incarnate* (IVP, 1977).
Cochrane, A. C. (ed.), *Reformed Confessions of the Sixteenth Century* (SCM, 1966).
Cullmann, O., *The Christology of the New Testament* (SCM, 1959).
Cupitt, D., *The Debate about Christ* (SCM, 1979).
Dunn, J. D. G., *Christology in the Making* (SCM, 1980).
Ebeling, G., *The Nature of Faith* (Collins, 1961).
Flesseman, E., *Geloven vandaag* (Callenbach, 1972).

France, R. T., 'The worship of Jesus: a neglected factor in Christological debate?' in Harold H. Rowdon (ed.), *Christ the Lord* (IVP, 1982).

Frey, C., *Dogmatik* (Gerd Mohn, 1977).

Fuller, D. P., *Easter Faith and History* (Tyndale Press, 1965).

Fuller, R. H., *The New Testament in Current Study* (Collins, 1962).

— *The Foundations of New Testament Christology* (Lutterworth, 1965).

Galot, J., *Who is Christ? A Theology of the Incarnation* (Gregorian University Press, 1981).

Goulder, M. (ed.), *Incarnation and Myth* (SCM, 1979).

Green, M. (ed.), *The Truth of God Incarnate* (Hodder, 1977).

Grillmeier, A., *Christ in Christian Tradition* (Mowbrays, ²1975).

Harnack, A. von, *The History of Dogma* 1 (Dover Publications, 1894).

— *What is Christianity?* (William & Norgate, ³1904).

Hartwell, H., *The Theology of Karl Barth: an Introduction* (Duckworth, 1964).

Hebblethwaite, B., 'The propriety of the doctrine of the Incarnation as a way of interpreting Christ' in *Scottish Journal of Theology* 33, June 1980.

Hengel, M., *The Son of God* (SCM, 1976).

Hick, J., *God and the Universe of Faith* (Macmillan, 1973).

— (ed.), *The Myth of God Incarnate* (SCM, 1977).

Jeremias, J., *New Testament Theology* 1 (SCM, 1971).

Jüngel, E., *God as the Mystery of the World: On the Foundation of the Theology of the Crucified One in the Dispute between Theism and Atheism* (Eerdmans, 1983).

Käsemann, E., *Essays on New Testament Themes* (SCM, 1964).

Klappert, B. (ed.), *Diskussion um Kreuz und Auferstehung* (Aussaat Verlag, 1967).

Kuitert, H. M., *The Reality of Faith* (Eerdmans, 1968).

Küng, H., *On Being a Christian* (Collins, Fount, 1978).

— *Does God Exist?* (Collins, 1980).

Ladd, G. E., *The New Testament and Criticism* (Hodder, 1967).

Lampe, G. W. H., 'The Holy Spirit and the Person of Christ' in S. W. Sykes and J. P. Clayton (eds.), *Christ, Faith and History* (CUP, 1972).

MacKinnon, D. M., 'The relation of the doctrines of the Incarnation and the Trinity' in Richard W. A. McKinney (ed.), *Creation, Christ and Culture* (T. & T. Clark, 1976).

Macquarrie, J., 'The Chalcedonian definition' in *The Expository Times* vol. 91, December 1979.

Marshall, I. H., *The Origins of New Testament Christology* (IVP, 1976).

— 'Incarnational Christology in the New Testament' in Harold H. Rowdon (ed.), *Christ the Lord* (IVP, 1982).

Martin, R. P., 'Some reflections on New Testament hymns' in Harold H. Rowdon (ed.), *Christ the Lord* (IVP, 1982).

Marxsen, W., *The Resurrection of Jesus of Nazareth* (SCM, 1970).

— *The Beginnings of Christology* (Fortress, 1979).

Mascall, E., *Theology and the Gospel of Christ* (SPCK, 1977).

Moltmann, J., *Theology of Hope* (SCM, 1967).

— *The Crucified God* (SCM, 1974).

— *The Trinity and the Kingdom of God* (SCM, 1981).

Moule, C. F. D., *The Origin of Christology* (CUP, 1977).
— (ed.), *The Significance of the Message of the Resurrection for Faith in Jesus Christ* (SCM, 1968).
Olive, D. H., *Wolfhart Pannenberg* (Word Books, 1973).
Pannenberg, W., *Jesus: God and Man* (SCM, 1968).
Pittenger, W. N., *God in Process* (SCM, 1967).
— *Christology Reconsidered* (SCM, 1970).
Prestige, G. L., *God in Patristic Thought* (SPCK, 1952).
Ridderbos, H., *Studies in Scripture and its Authority* (SPCK, 1978).
Robinson, J., and Cobb, J. B. (eds.), *Theology and History, New Frontiers in Theology* 3 (Harper and Row, 1967).
Robinson, J. A. T., *Honest to God* (SCM, 1963).
— *The Human Face of God* (SCM, 1973).
Runia, K., 'Karl Barth's Christology' in Harold H. Rowdon (ed.), *Christ the Lord* (IVP, 1982).
Schillebeeckx, E., *Jesus, An Experiment in Christology* (Collins, 1979).
— *Christ, The Christian Experience in the Modern World* (SCM, 1979).
— *Interim Report on the books 'Jesus' and 'Christ'* (SCM, 1980).
Schmithals, W., *An Introduction to the Theology of Rudolf Bultmann* (SCM, 1968).
Schweitzer, A.,*The Quest of the Historical Jesus* (Black, ³1954).
Schoonenberg, P., *The Christ* (Sheed & Ward, 1972).
Sellers, R. V., *The Council of Chalcedon* (SPCK, 1952).
Stott, J. R. W., 'Is the Incarnation a Myth?' in *Christianity Today*, November 4, 1977.
Tappert, T. G. (ed.), *The Book of Concord. The Confessions of the Evangelical Lutheran Church* (Fortress, 1959).
Tupper, E. F., *The Theology of Wolfhart Pannenberg* (Westminster, 1973).
Walker, W., *A History of the Christian Church* (T. & T. Clark, ³1976).
Wiles, M. F., *The Remaking of Christian Doctrine* (SCM, 1974).
Wilken, R. L., *The Myth of Christian Beginnings* (SCM, 1979).
Zamoyta, V., *A Theology of Christ: Sources* (Bruce, 1967).

Index